THE NATIONAL INSTITUTE OF
ECONOMIC AND SOCIAL RESEARCH

Occasional Papers

XXV

THE ANALYSIS AND FORECASTING OF THE BRITISH ECONOMY

THE NATIONAL INSTITUTE OF ECONOMIC AND SOCIAL RESEARCH

2 DEAN TRENCH STREET, SMITH SQUARE
LONDON, SWIP 3HE

The National Institute of Economic and Social Research is an independent, non-profit-making body, founded in 1938. It has as its aim the promotion of realistic research, particularly in the field of economics. It conducts research by its own research staff and in co-operation with the universities and other academic bodies. The results of the work done under the Institute's auspices are published in several series, and a list of its publications up to the present time will be found at the end of this volume.

THE ANALYSIS AND FORECASTING OF THE BRITISH ECONOMY

BY

M. J. C. SURREY

CAMBRIDGE
AT THE UNIVERSITY PRESS
1971

CONTENTS

TABLES

CHARTS

CONVENTIONS AND SYMBOLS

Regression equations from other sources are generally in the same notation as in the original: it was not possible to standardise the form of presentation. Correlation coefficients, standard errors of the regression coefficients (in brackets underneath) and of the residuals, also a measure of the serial correlation (the Durbin-Watson statistic) are given wherever available.

The following is the notation used in equations etc. which have not previously been published and where no other definitions are given (italics indicate current prices, all other values are at constant prices):

CE = consumers' expenditure
CEND = consumers' non-credit expenditure
CG = *current grants to persons*
CPI = consumer price index
CPIFC = consumer price index net of indirect tax content
CR = *consumer credit* (hire purchase or bank debt)
DNI = *income from dividends and net interest receipts*
E = employment
EEC = *employees' contributions to National Insurance*
ERC = *employers' contributions to private superannuation schemes*
EX = exports of goods and services
FCA = adjustment to factor cost
FP = *forces' pay*
GDP = gross domestic product
GFI = gross fixed investment
IMP = imports of goods and services
INV = stockbuilding
IRSE = *income from rent and self-employment*
MP = import prices
NI = *net insurance contributions* (*ERC* less *EEC*)
NTA = *net transfers abroad*
OPI = *other personal income* (other than wages and salaries and current grants)
PAC = public authorities' consumption
PDI = personal disposable income
RPDI = real personal disposable income
made up of: RDW = real disposable wage and salary income
RDO = other real disposable income
S = level of stocks
T = indirect tax component of consumer prices

TAX = *personal income tax payments*
made up of: *TAXWS* = *tax on wages and salaries*
TAXO = *tax on other incomes*
TFS = total final sales
TIM = time
TPI = *total personal income*
ULC = *unit labour costs* (*WS*/GDP)
WR = wage rates
WS = *wage and salary bill*

In equations:

Δ (Greek delta) is used for the change in a variable.
Negative subscripts are used for quarterly lags, e.g. E_{-1} is employment lagged one quarter.
t is a quarterly time-trend.

In tables:

— means zero.
. . means not available.

Roman numerals are used to indicate quarters of the calendar year, e.g. 1959 IV for the fourth quarter of 1959.

AUTHOR'S PREFACE

This book is an account of the present stage of work which has been developed over more than a dozen years, to which successive members of the Institute's staff have contributed directly and indirectly. It would be quite impossible to acknowledge them all by name. The planning of this study was undertaken by the Deputy Director, Dr C. A. Blyth and the Editor of the *Economic Review*, Mr M. J. Artis. The Introduction has been written by the Director, Mr G. D. N. Worswick, and the appendix describing the computing programme by Mr J. A. Bispham. The development of the particular model described owed a great deal to the work of Messrs I. G. Black and J. E. Kidgell. The Secretary, Mrs K. Jones, organised the publication, Mrs G. I. Barlow prepared the text for the printer and Miss M. Acland-Hood compiled the index.

I should like to thank Sir Donald MacDougall, Mr A. D. Roy and their colleagues of the Treasury, for a most thorough and helpful reading of the first draft of the paper; also Lord Roberthall and other members of the Institute's Executive Committee, and Mr F. T. Blackaby, Mr W. A. H. Godley and Mr K. A. Griffin for valuable comments.

The *Economic Review* was launched with a five-year grant from the Ford Foundation and supported by contributions from British companies and banks. Since 1966 the Social Science Research Council has made grants towards the cost of research and editorial work for the *Review*. Grants from the Treasury have never been made for the *Review* itself but have been available for fundamental research in the forecasting field. All these grants and contributions towards the research described in this paper are gratefully acknowledged.

London, March 1971 M.J.C.S.

INTRODUCTION

BY G. D. N. WORSWICK

This Occasional Paper contains an account of a model of the British economy which is currently used by a team of economists at the National Institute of Economic and Social Research to assist them in preparing the analyses and forecasts published at quarterly intervals in the *National Institute Economic Review*. The specifications of relationships and the methods of estimation used will be seen to be familiar. The paper makes no claim to originality so far as economic theory and econometric method are concerned.

The main reason for publishing this paper is to fill a gap in the literature on how the National Institute goes about its forecasts. The analyses and forecasts of the *Economic Review* attract considerable publicity, and with it come enquiries of all kinds about methods used and estimates made on particular occasions. It has always been the practice of the Institute team to answer such enquiries and, more generally, in presenting their work to put their cards on the table. It is in this spirit, for example, that the main tables for gross domestic product and the balance of payments give detailed figures, quarter by quarter over the forecast period, for the principal components. This is not because it is possible to forecast with such apparent precision the movement of any of these components from one quarter to the next a full year ahead. On the contrary some tables are headed with a note to the effect: 'The forecast figures are ... not intended to be more precise than the general statements in the text.' The tables are really the work-sheets of the Institute team. In the text the editor can make all the necessary qualifications surrounding any particular forecast. The reason for publishing the work-sheet figures is to assist the serious reader to check through, step by step, the way in which the analysis has been made and the forecast built up, and to allow him to work out the numerical consequences of substituting his own judgements in particular places for those of the Institute. It also enables the reader to verify how well or badly earlier forecasts have turned out.

In the same way an attempt is made to be completely open about methodology. With the aid of the small print in footnotes and special articles which appear from time to time, it should be possible for a very assiduous student to reproduce for himself many of the calculations. With the passage of time, however, these calculations have become increasingly complex, and a newcomer would now find it a major job to work his way through back numbers in order to distil the essence of the methods.

A short general account of the Institute's methods has already been published,[1] but the present paper brings together descriptions in much greater detail of the component parts of the forecasting process as it has recently been carried out. We hope that this will be of service to those who already make use of the *Economic Review*. We hope also that the book will be of interest to teachers of economics. Too often economic theory and statistical methods and sources are kept separate. If this book can lay any claim to novelty it is in the way in which theory and measurement are kept together throughout. It is especially with this pedagogic aspect in mind that we have included, in an appendix, a 'do it yourself' kit for the operation of the econometric model.

The greater part of the paper is taken up in describing an economic model which is used in short-term economic forecasting. The two things are not the same. The making and operation of the model is only one part of the process of forecasting which extends in many directions, both preceding and following the operation of the model itself. An attempt is made in chapter 9 to outline the forecasting process and to indicate where the economic model fits in. The proportion of the pages in this book devoted to the description of the model should not be taken as a measure of its importance in the forecasting process. Some experienced forecasters would still maintain that the judgement of the forecaster considerably outweighs the influence of any differences in the size and sophistication of mechanical aids, such as econometric models, which he may use. But whereas the latter can be described in detail there is not a great deal which can be said about acquiring the former.

The word forecast conveys the ideas of prediction and of planning or contrivance. The ordinary man regards a weather forecast as a prediction. The element of planning comes in the use of the forecast as an aid in deciding whether to take an umbrella. In economics there is an analogy with this at the micro level. A particular firm may take a forecast of sales for the industry as a datum, and make its own plans accordingly. But whereas the outcome of a forecast of rain is unaffected by the number of people who put up umbrellas, the outcome of a forecast of a rise in national product could be affected by the number of firms who believed it and altered their investment and stockbuilding plans accordingly. There is a further difference. A forecast that, with present policies unchanged, there will be a substantial increase in unemployment might well lead the authorities to take action to prevent it happening. In economic and social affairs adaptation to events and control of events are more closely intertwined with the events themselves than in the physical world, and this has an important influence upon the way in which forecasts are presented. A government or a central bank might like to have the forecast in the form of the expected

[1] M. J. Artis, 'Short-term economic forecasting at NIESR' in K. Hilton and D. F. Heathfield (eds.), *The Econometric Study of the United Kingdom*, London, Macmillan, 1970.

development of the economy on the assumption of unchanged policies, or it might ask for a series of alternative forecasts based on different assumptions about policies, for example tax changes. An industrialist might be less concerned with what will happen if the government does nothing, than with whether the government will act and if so which of the possible measures it will choose. The National Institute forecasts are usually made for a period up to twenty-four months ahead on the assumption of 'unchanged policies'. This means, for example, that present tax rates are taken as given, unless changes to be made at some future date have already been announced. Similarly for credit regulations and for government expenditure. For monetary policy, it is necessary to make an assumption about the future degree of strictness which is in accordance with what is known of present policy. This form of presentation clearly helps informed opinion to take a critical view of economic policy, and this is one of the objectives of the *Economic Review*.[1] But, as was suggested above, it might appear to be not the best form for an individual enterprise, which could prefer a well-informed estimate of what is likely to happen to a forecast of what would happen if the government took no action. However the forecast is usually presented in such a way that it is possible for the reader to insert his own guesses about political decisions and thus to deduce his own 'total' or unconditional forecast. Indeed there is a strong case for maintaining the form of the conditional forecast. Economic forecasting is admittedly rudimentary and its successes have been only moderate, but the art or science of political forecasting seems to be cruder still. This is one reason, though of course not the only one, for presenting the economic forecast in terms, explicitly or implicitly, of alternatives or choices, without going on to predict how those choices are likely to be made.

The original purpose of the forecast was, and remains, to produce a consistent set of quarterly estimates for the recent past and the immediate future of the principal components of national income, such as consumption, investment, exports and imports. The consistency sought is of two kinds: the first requires that the rules of accounting should be maintained within any and every time period, and the second requires that the relationships between different variables within and between periods should be consistent with various postulated structural equations. In its bare

[1] The particular form of presentation of the Institute's analysis reflects the fact that the Institute's forecasting was undertaken in the first place, in 1959, in response to the initiative of Sir Robert Hall (now Lord Roberthall), then Economic Adviser to the Treasury, who wished to see another team of economists making national income forecasts and conducting research into methods of improving them. This would provide a second opinion on the state of the economy, besides the unpublished one which Treasury officials were putting forward to ministers. It was also thought that research might more easily be undertaken in an outside body than in a department responsible for day to day administration. For a fuller account of the origins of the National Institute forecasts see the article by Lord Roberthall in the *National Institute Economic Review*, No. 50, November 1969.

essentials the forecasting process has changed relatively little. The first step is to make estimates of the probable changes in certain 'exogenous' or primary variables, notably investment, exports, import prices and public expenditure, and to derive the remaining 'endogenous' variables, such as consumption and the volume of imports, by using a model, which is, in its essentials, a lagged multiplier combined with an 'accelerator' for stock-building. In detail, however, the methods both of forecasting the exogenous variables and of deducing the endogenous variables have been subject to continuous change and development, usually, though not invariably, in the direction of greater technical sophistication. In the past two years the economic model, which was always implicit, if somewhat informally, in the forecasting process, has been formalised in such a manner that estimates of the consequences of altering one or more of the exogenous variables can be obtained with great rapidity from the electronic computer. It is this present model which is the subject of the greater part of this paper.

The perceptive reader will have noticed that in describing this development of the forecasting method the word 'improvement' was not used. There can be no doubt that the methods currently in use are distinctly more sophisticated than those of ten years ago. There is nevertheless room for debate on whether they have resulted in any significant improvement in predictive performance.

On the face of it, the method to find out whether forecasts have improved is to apply a battery of tests to forecasts made, say, five or ten years ago, and to compare the results with those obtained by applying the same tests to forecasts made more recently. This looks straightforward enough, but in practice the business of testing forecasts is as difficult as forecasting itself and shares many of its uncertainties. It is essential to understand why this is so before one can appreciate the status of the present model in the totality of the forecasting process.

The first question to decide is what exactly is to be tested. Forecasts are often made with the aid of econometric relationships, but not without qualification. The figure indicated by the equation may be adjusted by the forecaster in the light of special factors present at the time of making the forecast. Whether it is the equation alone which is being tested, or the forecast, consisting of the equation plus judgement, several tests are likely to be required since a single test might come out right by chance. If we are testing the equation alone it is possible to provide a number of tests. If, for example, we have time-series for a number of variables covering the period t_0 to t_n, we can break the period arbitrarily at t_r, estimate the parameters of an equation connecting the variables from the data for the period t_0 to t_r, and use the equation to 'predict' values for the dependent variable in t_{r+1} to t_n, which can then be compared with the (already known) actual values for the same sub-period. Even with this ability to chop up the past, it may not always be possible to guarantee a sufficient number of tests to show convincingly that equation *A* performs systematically better than equation *B*. Very often all that statistical tests will do is to reject some equations but still leave an embarrassingly large choice of explanatory options in play.

For the testing of complete forecasts (equations plus judgement) this recourse to the device of predicting the already known past is not available. Even with equations it is difficult enough to prevent one's knowledge of what actually did happen during the test period from influencing the form of equation, which ought to be specified on the basis of the observations in the estimation period alone. To attempt to re-enact just how one would have exercised judgement in adjusting any particular equation in the past is simply not practicable. This means that in testing forecasts one is obliged to resort to actual, and not simulated, forecasts; but the number of such forecasts available may be too few to permit any very exacting tests. For example the National Institute has produced forecasts at quarterly intervals. To test whether the forecasting has improved we would hardly be satisfied with the evidence of a single forecast using a new method. Suppose that we would be satisfied with the average performance on twelve occasions, which is still statistically very small. This would enable us to ascertain whether present forecasting is better than it was five years ago; however it would be quite possible that methods had lately taken a turn for the worse, but it would be three years at least before one could pick up this trend.

The second problem is that, in the *Economic Review*, national income forecasts are not unconditional, but are, as we have already seen, projections made on the basis of 'unchanged policies'. Such forecasts, whether in the *Review* or from the government's own advisers, are sometimes warning signals, and it may well be that action is taken within the forecast period to forestall the outcome foreseen in the original forecast. In such circumstances it would be perverse to compare the actual out-turn directly with the original forecast. What is first necessary is some allowance for the effect upon the outcome of the change in policy induced by the original forecast. Where, as in the present case, a complete model of the economy has been developed, this should present no logical difficulty. Just as the model is used to derive the forecast from certain assumed values of the exogenous variables, so also can the model be used to work out the effect of a change in policy, for example a tax change. There is nothing procedurally wrong, as some people appear to think, in using the *same* method to 'correct' the forecast as was used to derive it in the first place, if that method is still the best available.[1] The difficulty is not one of logic, but simply that if the

[1] Of course if the testing of forecasts is being done some years after the event, then it may well be that biases have been detected in the method or model originally used and have now been corrected in the current model. In these circumstances the correction for policy changes in the original year should be made with the latest model and not with the one which was used for the

'corrected' forecast still differs from the actual out-turn, then there may be no practical way of deciding how much of this error should be attributed to an error in the original forecast and how much to an error in the correction.

The third difficulty is that many of the estimates of economic variables which are to hand at the time of the forecast may subsequently be revised. There are many reasons for such revisions and their scale can sometimes be quite substantial. To give but one example, twice in the last two years we have been informed of systematic under-recording of exports to the extent of 2 per cent. Some revisions are virtually inevitable: official statisticians have to make some working compromise between accuracy, which frequently requires time, and speed. One ought to be very suspicious of a statistical system which publishes first estimates which are never subsequently altered.

By the middle of the year a forecaster may have to hand the first estimate of the national product in the first quarter of that year, call it Y_1, and he may predict that it will be F_1 in the first quarter of the following year.[1] Then at first sight all we have to do is to wait a year and observe whether the national product indeed turns out to be F_1. But all sorts of possibilities now arise. The first, which hardly ever happens, is that both Y_1 and F_1, which are the first estimates published by the Central Statistical Office, are also the final ones in the sense that they are never subsequently changed: in this case there is no difficulty in deciding whether the forecast is good or not. Much more likely, however, by the time we come to look at the size of F, is that the original figure for Y will have been changed upwards or downwards to Y_2. Let us suppose that our initial observation of F was F_2, which is not equal to the forecast F_1. We might then notice that, although the level of the forecast of national product has proved incorrect, the difference $F_2 - Y_2$ was equal to $F_1 - Y_1$; that is to say we had correctly forecast the change from one year to the next. Which then is the test to be applied? Should we compare the forecast levels or the forecast changes? Going forward a further year we may find that the figures in the Blue Book are now respectively Y_3 and F_3, and we may further notice that, in terms of changes, the forecast now appears in a somewhat better light than it did when first tested. Should we regard this as a vindication of the forecasting method?

This raises the question whether the object is to forecast the value for F (or $F-Y$) which the official statisticians will give next year, or to forecast

---

original forecast. In short, whether for making a forecast or for making corrections for changes in policy, one uses the best model available at the time of making the forecast or the time of making the adjustment.

[1] In this example we set aside the complications introduced by changes of policy within the period of the forecast.

the 'truth', to which next year's official estimate will be the first approximation, liable to subsequent revision. One is inclined to answer that it is the latter: indeed it is arguable that the forecaster should be prepared to query the official estimate of a particular variable, if he considers it to be out of line with estimates of other variables in the light of his knowledge of the structure of the economy. Unfortunately we may never know with absolute certainty what the 'truth' about any particular year actually was. Revisions to estimates may still be made several years after the event. At the time it is made each revision may be supposed to be better than the figure it replaces because it is based on more or later information, but inspection of the successive revisions does not disclose an invariable pattern of asymptotic movement towards the final estimate. Thus the forecaster is in the uncomfortable position that it may not be known for some years whether he was right about where he was starting from, or right about where he thought the economy was going.[1] The importance of this problem obviously depends upon the size and frequency of revisions. In the British case revisions can be as large as 1 per cent and sometimes more, in variables which are not changing by more than 3 to 5 per cent in any one year, and revisions may still be made some years after the event.

A special aspect of this problem is that there are different estimates for changes in real gross domestic product according to whether it is approached along the income, expenditure or output routes. Sometimes the change from one quarter to the next shown by one such indicator, say the expenditure estimate, may be in a different direction from that shown by another, perhaps the income measure. The Central Statistical Office says that, in general, there is no reason for preferring one of these measures to another, although on particular occasions there may be reasons for thinking that a particular one is the most reliable: consequently it is thought that the best representation of the movement of the economy is given by 'compromise GDP' – an average of the three separate estimates, which to date has been the arithmetic mean. The use of compromise GDP, however, raises a tricky problem of the disposal of the difference between this measure and, for example, gross domestic expenditure, since the national accounts are set out in such a way as to add up to the latter and not the former. This question is discussed later in the book (see appendix 1): it is mentioned here simply to indicate yet another source of difficulty in comparing a forecast with the actual out-turn.

The final difficulty comes from a rather simple ambiguity in the expression 'economic forecast'. This could refer either to the forecast for a single variable or, as is the sense when we speak of a Treasury forecast or a National Institute forecast, a series of estimates for a number of variables, usually on a quarterly basis, for a specified number of quarters ahead.

[1] This does not, of course, preclude the making of provisional tests.

If, first of all, we are testing success in the forecasting of a particular variable, say exports, one simple way to proceed might be to compare the change from the fourth quarter of one year to the fourth quarter of the next as shown in the original forecast and as subsequently observed. This is a simple method and, if repeated for a series of forecasts, it allows one to take averages and to study the range of error in the forecast. Nevertheless the forecaster might complain that such a test does not do justice to what forecasting is about. He might say that he is not trying to pin down precisely the value of exports or any other variable in one particular quarter, but rather to pick up the general movement of the variable concerned.

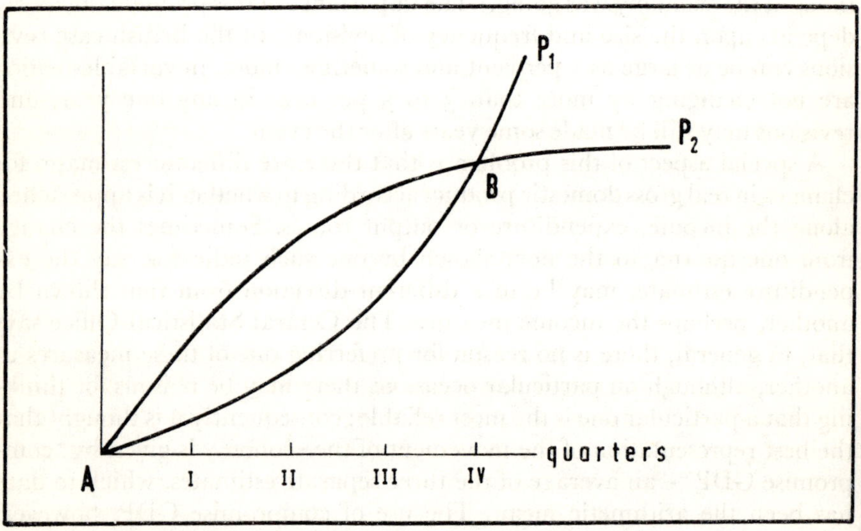

In the diagram the alternative paths for the economy, P_1 and P_2, show the same change from the fourth quarter of one year to the fourth quarter of the next, yet they clearly constitute very different forecasts. To characterise such a forecast, a single number, namely the change from fourth quarter to fourth quarter, is insufficient. If we postulated that the forecast belonged to a family of quadratics passing through A and B we would need one additional number to characterise it. If we postulated a cubic, which would allow us to represent initial acceleration followed by subsequent deceleration, two additional values would be required, and so on. More elaborate tests could in principle be constructed, so that the success of the forecast could itself be submitted to statistical study. But instead of one average and a range of errors for a single value, we should now have two or more averages with corresponding ranges of errors, and the question whether one set of forecasts was better than another would no longer be unambiguous. Moreover, the more numbers we use up in order to characterise any particular forecast, the larger is the sample of forecasts needed to obtain any given degree of significance in comparing one sample with another.

The other problem is that, in a forecast of a set of variables, each of them is not of equal importance, nor are the variables which, from a policy point of view, are the most important now necessarily the ones which will be most important five years hence. There may be times when unemployment is more important than any other single variable, other times when the balance of payments dominates, and yet other times when the change in the price level is the matter for most concern. One could overcome this formally by specifying some 'testing function', which would give weights to the forecasting errors of the different variables, the weights themselves being adjusted according to the shifting policy significance of the variables. But while such a formal procedure can be described, it may make very little sense when the number of forecasts with which one is concerned is small.

Sufficient has been said to show that the testing of forecasts, and of econometric aids to forecasting, is by no means so straightforward as might appear at first sight. While it is always possible to construct formal testing procedures, it does not follow that they will yield definitive answers to such questions as: 'Is method *A* superior to method *B*?' or 'Has this team of forecasters become better since they started?'[1]

We have been concerned so far with the question whether one can establish that forecasting has improved or not. There is a different question whether forecasting is worthwhile in some absolute sense. Some sceptics have suggested that economic forecasts of the kind undertaken by the National Institute are not worth having, such attacks being based predominantly on comparisons with so-called 'naïve' forecasting devices of a purely statistical character. In the simplest case for example, the economic forecaster's record of prediction of GDP changes is compared with the predictions reached from following a rule such as 'same change as last year'. When the naïve prediction rule produces smaller errors on average than the economic forecaster's predictions, it is claimed that the case for *economic*

[1] Two analyses of the Institute's forecasts have been published: M. C. Kennedy, 'How well does the National Institute forecast?', *National Institute Economic Review*, No. 50, November 1969, and R. L. Major and M. J. C. Surrey, 'Errors in National Institute forecasts of the balance of payments', *National Institute Economic Review*, No. 52, May 1970. These articles indicate the scale of errors and nature of biases in Institute forecasting.

forecasting is weakened if not destroyed. More complicated naïve models of a purely statistical kind can be employed, very frequently making use of auto-regressive schemes.

What conclusion as to the reliability of economic forecasts can be drawn from such comparisons is rather debatable. With ingenuity it is usually possible to construct some complex auto-regressive scheme which will fit pretty accurately to the relatively regular cyclical fluctuations of many variables in the British economy in the past fifteen years. With the additional benefit of hindsight, and bearing in mind the fairly small number of forecasts actually recorded, it should not prove too difficult to design such a scheme to beat any set of forecasts. The important question, however, is whether, turning once more to the future, such a critic would be prepared to base his policy upon the movement of the economy indicated by the auto-regressive scheme rather than that reached by some 'economic' method of forecasting. Some economists do have the courage of their convictions in this respect. Professor Milton Friedman's rule concerning fixed annual increments of the money supply would appear to be such an instance. Others will take courage from the fact that there is a fair amount of evidence that economic forecasting has performed somewhat better than coin tossing.

In any case the question whether forecasting as such should be undertaken cannot seriously be at issue. Where the absolute level of performance of economic forecasting is important is in indicating the frontiers of feasibility in economic management.

It is not possible, for the reasons above, to guide the research programme in a wholly scientific manner, adopting procedures which have been performed well in tests and rejecting those which have not. Testing is necessary, but by no means always conclusive. Nevertheless there can be discerned a distinct trend in the research programme towards the introduction of formal econometric relationships, and towards the elaboration of formal economic models for the whole economy and sub-models for the particular sectors, such as exports. It is true that there is always likely to remain an element of personal judgement in economic forecasting, but wherever it is possible for private judgement to be satisfactorily replaced by public procedures this should be done. In this way the scientific foundations upon which judgements will still have to be made can be continuously strengthened. In recent years the possibilities of generating public procedures have been powerfully assisted by the electronic computer and by an increasing supply of young economists trained to use it. There are, it is true, dangers that the ability to make almost limitless regressions can sometimes drive out careful thought and commonsense. On the other hand, formalising hitherto intuitive procedures can bring out aspects of these procedures which, without the aid of the computer, might never have been discovered at all.

Anyone acquainted with contemporary econometric model building will be struck by the smallness of the Institute's present model.[1] There are several reasons for this. The first is historical: in its essentials the present model formalises procedures which have been evolving since the Institute began work in this field, in contrast with many econometric models which are constructed from scratch and which tend to incorporate more equations.[2] Secondly, it contains non-linear relationships, which have created difficulties in the writing of a suitable programme—difficulties which might be increased if the model were larger. Thirdly, any model which is to be used regularly has to be continuously maintained, for the structural parameters of the economy are by no means as stable and unchanging as some text books might lead us to expect. Each equation has to be continuously monitored for its performance, and where equations have broken down new ones must be put in, or new parts of the whole model redesigned. Five years ago the Institute team would have claimed that the relationships between output, employment and unemployment were pretty well understood and satisfactorily embodied in a set of equations, from which a good estimate could be derived of the underlying growth of productive potential in the economy. They are much less confident today. There has been some kind of shift in the significance of the unemployment statistic in relation to other economic indicators, particularly in connection with the expected movement of wages and prices. Until two years ago the Institute relied upon Phillips type relationships, but if unemployment is used in such relationships now they are clearly wrong (1970–1): the unemployment percentage is higher than it has been at any time since the end of the Second War, but, instead of being at very low levels, the rates of increase of both money wage rates and money earnings are higher than ever before.

This is not the place to discuss the reasons for the breakdown or shift in

[1] It would be more exact to speak of the 'kernel' of the econometric model, which takes the value of the exogenous variables such as exports as predetermined. In fact, considerable research effort has been devoted to constructing econometric sub-models for some of the exogenous variables, but these sub-models are not directly plugged in to the kernel. The predicted values yielded by the sub-models are set side by side with forecasts made by less formal methods and the best forecast is reached by the exercise of judgement. The smallness of the kernel should not, however, be taken as a measure of the extent to which econometric relationships are used in the complete forecasting process.

[2] In fact the Institute's own first systematic attempt in this field was of this latter kind. That is to say, the forecasting team decided on the ambitious task of constructing an entirely new linear model, in which all relationships would be estimated by the appropriate procedures, and which would allow a considerably greater degree of disaggregation than was previously incorporated in the partial relationships and permit special attention to be paid to the problem of estimation of the parameters. The results of that experiment can be found in a paper by R. P. Byron in Hilton and Heathfield (eds.), *The Econometric Study of the United Kingdom*. When it was tested, however, the performance of this model was very poor and it became apparent that there would be enormous difficulties in getting it to work. It was decided, therefore, to re-examine the problem of 'computerising' the existing forecasting methods, which had previously been rejected on the grounds that some of the forecasting relationships were non-linear.

relationships of this kind. The point is that they have occurred and they will occur again. Ideally one might envisage the process of model building as a journey through the economy in which successive structural relationships were firmly pinned down by research, so that a model increasing in size and sensitivity could be steadily constructed. As it turns out, even the most basic relationships need constant attention and patching up or complete replacement. Thus there is introduced into the model-building procedure the overriding need for flexibility. There are then serious obstacles in the way of expanding the model, but subject to the availability of finance they are not insuperable, and there are a number of directions in which extension would appear *prima facie* to be desirable. It has often been said, for example, that the Institute's model is deficient in that it leaves out money. This is not altogether correct. To the extent that changes in the money supply impinge upon the economy at large, there must be some transmission mechanism. One of the routes is through its influence upon fixed investment expenditure, through a change in either the cost or the availability of credit. In so far as the investment forecast takes into account the results of surveys of investment intentions, this particular monetary effect is already allowed for, in part at least. Another route for transmission is through consumer expenditure and here the monetary influence turns up directly in what is called the 'credit effect'. It is in fact the case that a monetary variable, for example an interest variable, has frequently been included in one or other of the structural equations, only for it to turn out that the coefficient is not statistically significant so that the variable has been dropped. Nevertheless the opportunity is now arising for more intensive research in the monetary field in the United Kingdom. The Radcliffe Committee reporting in 1959 included recommendations for the extension of financial statistics which were duly taken up by the Central Statistical Office and the Bank of England. This has led to a supply of statistics without which the incorporation of monetary factors into a quarterly model was previously impossible. The development of a model of the monetary sector is one possible line of extension. Nor is it difficult to draw up quite a long list of other areas in which one might hope that further research would yield returns.

The construction and operation of the econometric model is a part, but not the whole, of the process of economic forecasting. It would probably not be very fruitful to try to estimate just how much the model contributes – whether the major part or the minor part – so long as it is recognised that it is only a part, and that there is an important remainder consisting of processes which involve an element of private judgement and which cannot, as yet or at all, be reduced to formal public procedures. The statistical data need to be scrutinised in order to tease out, if one can, the effects of special factors, for example, dock strikes, import surcharges and so on;

where economic indicators point in different directions reasons must be sought for preferring one to the other; and all the time care must be taken that adjustments in one part of the model do not entail logical inconsistencies.

One consequence of the process of continuous modification and adaptation of the model is that the version presented in these pages will already be partly obsolete, so far as current National Institute use is concerned, by the time this paper is published. The obsolescence may be minor – for example, a particular equation may still be in its same form but the coefficients will have become different because of re-estimation with revised data – or it may be on a major scale involving the replacement of one equation with several or, as has happened in the past, the collapse of several equations into one.

It was mentioned above that the idea that the National Institute should undertake economic forecasting originated with Treasury economists. There have been other links with the Treasury. Some members of the original Institute team had had previous Treasury experience before 1959. From 1963 to 1965 Mr Wynne Godley, then of the Treasury, was seconded to the Institute to develop research in this field and the model expounded here still bears traces of his work. The author of the present book, Mr Surrey, had himself worked in the Treasury before he came to the Institute. There has also been movement the other way of Institute members joining the Treasury. But although there have been, and we hope there will continue to be, links with the Treasury, they have been on a personal and informal basis. Both the Institute itself and the economic analysis and forecasting conducted by it are wholly independent. This cannot be emphasised too strongly. Some observers, especially abroad, find it hard to believe that the *Economic Review* is not in some way under the influence of the Treasury, if for no other purpose than to fly kites. But there is no substance in this. The *Economic Review* is published, so naturally the Treasury economists know what the Institute is up to, and from time to time there are discussions of technical questions in meetings and seminars, but the staff of the *Review* do not know any more about the Treasury's thinking and estimating at a particular moment than appears in official publications, in Hansard and in newspapers. Not only do they not know, but they would not wish to know. It is to be expected that two independent teams using basically similar methods would, from time to time, make closely similar forecasts. If they never did, the outlook for economic science would be bleak indeed. But there is much scope for different readings of the same data, based on differences of theory or different methods of estimating relationships. In bringing such differences out into the open and trying to trace their causes, progress can be made in improving economic forecasting. From this point of view the Institute's own methods might well be improved if more were known about what the Treasury actually does.[1] But against this must be set the serious risk of unconscious collusion, which could easily jeopardise one of the main purposes of the exercise, namely the giving of a wholly independent opinion on the state of the economy.[2]

[1] The present book is entirely concerned with methods used at the National Institute. The most recent published accounts of Treasury methods are: A. D. Roy, 'Short-term forecasting for central economic management of the UK economy' in Hilton and Heathfield (eds.), *The Econometric Study of the United Kingdom*, and J. R. Shepherd, 'Short-term forecasting for the UK economy' in Sir Alec Cairncross (ed.), *The Managed Economy*, Oxford, Basil Blackwell, 1970. Both papers describe the methods of 1969 and both list references.

[2] This is not intended as an argument against the publication of more of the Treasury forecast than already appears, annually, in the Financial Statement. Once such a forecast is published, the *Review* is free to accept it, or to reject it giving reasons for the disagreement. However, the government may well know some things, either facts or intentions, which it does not wish to disclose. In such circumstances it would be better for the *Review* to publish a possibly wrong forecast based on its own public knowledge, than to trim the forecast to allow for confidential information to which it could not refer.

CHAPTER I

THE ECONOMY IN OUTLINE

In what remains virtually the only attempt to give a comprehensive account of the macro-economic structure of the British economy, J. C. R. Dow wrote: 'At the present stage of the debate it hardly seems possible to do more than give reasons for selecting certain lines of causal interconnections as the main ones of importance; and to indicate, where possible, the probable magnitude of the responses.'[1] In the seven years since Dow's study appeared, the volume of econometric work on the British economy has been considerable, yet the greater part of this work has tended to lend precision to the 'magnitudes of the responses' rather than to change the selection of the main 'lines of causal interconnections'. This book is no exception, and the reader who seeks a more exhaustive treatment of the general picture than is presented here is referred to Dow's study.

The empirical work summarised here is that done at the National Institute. Where the results of such work have been published (normally in the *National Institute Economic Review*) only the main results are quoted; references are given for those who seek a fuller account. Where results have not been published some attempt is made to give a more complete summary. In no case is there any attempt to provide a survey of research done elsewhere, even where this has influenced the approach of research workers at the Institute.[2]

The analytic framework to be described deals in broad aggregates, generally in an economy-wide sense: exports, investment, consumption, and so on, relate to the economy as a whole and not to individual sectors or industries. Each of these aggregates represents a set of demands on economic resources; their sum represents, at a given time, the total demand on resources, which is supplied from domestic production and from imports of goods and services produced overseas. The level of domestic production is, of course, a major determinant of the level of employment.[3] The capacity of the economy to produce goods and services will grow over time as

[1] J. C. R. Dow, *The Management of the British Economy, 1945–60*, Cambridge University Press, 1964, p. 3.

[2] Mention must be made, however, of other attempts at the construction of full models of the economy – notably those of the London Business School, the University of Southampton, and an earlier model-building exercise at the National Institute. For descriptions of these models, see the contributions by J. R. Ball and T. Burns, Ivor Pearce, and R. P. Byron in Hilton and Heathfield (eds.), *The Econometric Study of the United Kingdom*.

[3] Those familiar with national accounting methods will be aware of the distinctions between gross and net product, and between domestic and national product. For a variety of (mainly statistical) reasons we work entirely with the gross concept of product and, because of our interest in the level of domestic employment, we use gross domestic rather than gross national product.

technical and managerial progress increase the productivity of given factor resources; it will also be affected by the rates of change of factor inputs – the supply of labour and the stock of capital. Actual output in relation to the level which would keep resources fully employed is often referred to, in general, as the 'pressure of demand'.[1] In general terms, and without the intention of begging questions to be raised later, the pressure of demand may be taken to affect unemployment, the overseas trade balance, the rate of inflation and other key policy variables. Output – gross domestic product (GDP) – is thus the central point of the whole framework.

Following the main lines of development of macro-economics since the appearance of Keynes's *General Theory*, the model is essentially demand-oriented.[2] Since the main interest is in demands on real resources, GDP and its components are measured at constant rather than at current prices. Quarterly figures, corrected for purely seasonal variation, are used throughout.

The expenditure account in the national accounting system is the starting point for the process of building a model of the economy. Taking 1969 as an example, table 1 shows the expenditure aggregates at constant (1963) prices, their relative sizes and their average rates of growth over the period 1958–69. It will be seen that over half of total final expenditure is accounted for by consumers' expenditure, while the remainder is made up, in roughly equal parts, by public consumption, exports and fixed investment. Stockbuilding is, in comparison, a very small proportion of final expenditure, but year-to-year *changes* in stockbuilding have been an important source of variations in the rate of growth of the total.

Of the total of final expenditure, less than three-quarters is met from domestic production as GDP.[3] Part of the remainder represents net indirect taxes and subsidies,[4] and nearly a fifth is met from imports.

For a complete account of these and other national accounting concepts and definitions, see Central Statistical Office, *National Accounts Statistics – Sources and Methods*, Rita Maurice (ed.), HMSO, 1968.

[1] The pressure of demand can be measured in several ways. Unemployment itself can be used as a simple proxy; some writers have used a measure which combines the levels of unemployment and of vacancies. A more complex measure is the ratio of actual output to productive potential or capacity (see below, chapter 7). The simplest measure of all is the ratio of output to its trend growth path, though this of course assumes that full-employment output grows with a steady trend.

[2] This is not to imply that the model is fully 'Keynesian'. In particular, there is at present no full monetary sector.

[3] The national accounts statisticians derive independent estimates of GDP from three separate sets of data: expenditures, incomes and output. To derive a single measure as used in the model, it is necessary to reconcile these three estimates; the method used is described below in appendix 1. This is only one of many data problems of a statistical kind. Of particular importance is the problem of revisions to national accounts and other data: this has implications in the estimation of relationships, and in both making and appraising forecasts. (See also the Introduction above and p. 64 below.)

[4] This needs some elaboration. Expenditures are most conveniently measured (and in all probability are economically determined) at market prices, that is inclusive of any indirect

Table 1. *Expenditure on the gross domestic product in 1969* [a]

	Value	Proportion of total final expenditure	Average annual growth rate, 1958–69
	£m.	%	%
Consumers' expenditure	22,629	52·2	2·6
Public authorities' current expenditure	5,800	13·4	2·2
Gross fixed investment	6,602	15·2	5·3
Exports of goods and services	8,055	18·6	4·6
equals: Total final sales	43,086	99·4	3·3
plus: Stockbuilding	276	0·6	
equals: Total final expenditure	43,362	100·0	3·3
less: Imports of goods and services	7,784	18·0	4·6
Adjustment to factor cost	4,252	9·8	3·6
equals: Gross domestic product (at factor cost)	31,326	72·2	3·0

SOURCE: Central Statistical Office, *National Income and Expenditure, 1969*, HMSO, 1970.

[a] At 1963 prices.

As it stands, table 1 shows simply one accounting identity. It also illustrates, however, part of the causal structure of a simple model of the economy. Other things being equal, a rise in consumption, or in exports, investment and so on, will raise the level of GDP, and a rise in imports will correspondingly lower it. But a large number of other causal links exist. Consumers' expenditure, for example, is principally determined by consumers' real incomes, so that a model must include the personal sector's income account, together with personal taxation. Again, since incomes are determined as money flows and not in real terms, an element of price

taxation associated with the goods and services in question. When prices indices are used to convert current price expenditures to base-year prices, these expenditures are thus implicitly being revalued inclusive of indirect taxes at base-year rates. But this indirect tax content does not, of course, represent a claim on resources; the factor cost adjustment is the sum of such contents, which must be subtracted from the total demands to give the total claim on real resources. When the portion of this claim which is met from overseas – imports – is deducted, the remainder represents the volume of total domestic output, usually referred to as GDP at base-year factor cost. In the present system of national accounts, base-year prices are those of 1963.

forecasting is needed in order to derive consumers' real incomes and hence their consumption. And since the balance of payments is presented in current price terms, explanations of the behaviour of import and export prices are required.

Many of these aspects involve causal links in the reverse direction from those immediately apparent from table 1. For example, although a rise in consumption will increase GDP, this will in turn raise employment incomes and hence consumption. Links of this kind make the system as a whole one of interdependent variables.

It was pointed out earlier that there are substantial areas where economic knowledge is inadequate or not relevant to the present framework. The elements of the national income affected must therefore be treated as exogenously determined. Public sector demands, for instance, are principally the result of government expenditure decisions rather than of well-understood economic forces. These demands thus cannot be explained within the model but must be fed in as data from outside. In practice, this distinction between exogenous and endogenous elements becomes blurred; in a very aggregated macro-economic model of the economy almost every element represents an heroic simplification of infinitely complex reality and the behaviour of each endogenous element must be regarded as determined not exclusively by the major influences presented in the behavioural relationships, but also by other influences which are omitted. In forecasting, it may be possible to guess at the likely effect of some of these influences and to introduce them as further 'exogenous' elements.[1]

AN INFORMAL DESCRIPTION OF THE MODEL

A working distinction is drawn between the behaviour of the domestic economy, centred round the level of domestic activity and cast predominantly in real terms, and the relationship between the domestic economy and the world economy, summarised in the balance of payments where money flows are most important. These two aspects are of course interdependent; in particular the level of exports, making up one large element in the balance of payments account, is also a determinant of the level of GDP, while the level of demand in the domestic economy is one of the principal determinants of the level of imports, another major element in the balance of payments.

Turning first to the domestic economy, the three main broad expenditure aggregates taken as being given exogenously (in the sense used above) are exports of goods and services, public authorities' current expenditure and public authorities' gross fixed investment. Other elements are taken as endogenous: for example, imports are related to total final sales and stock-

[1] This aspect of forecasting is discussed in detail in chapters 8 and 9 below.

building, stockbuilding to GDP, consumption to GDP (via an elaboration of the personal sector's income and expenditure accounts in which various other exogenous elements intrude) and indirect taxes to consumption. The system as a whole is thus one of simultaneous determination requiring a technique of simultaneous or iterative solution.[1]

For the past, when the model is used for descriptive and analytic purposes, the recorded levels of the exogenous elements are taken as data. In forecasting however, future levels must be predicted. *Exports of goods and services* are forecast with reference principally to the expected level and composition of world trade. Both total world trade and the share in it of British exports are complex to forecast. World trade is assumed to depend primarily on the rates of growth of output in different countries, so that output forecasts are needed for each of the major industrial countries, and a view has to be taken about likely economic conditions in the developed sterling area and the underdeveloped countries. Britain's share of world trade has fallen steadily but at a rate which has varied with the rate of growth of world trade. More formally, relationships have been developed between British exports of manufactures and industrial countries' output and imports, and between British exports to underdeveloped countries and those countries' financial position.[2] These relationships were all in terms of the value of exports, and a forecast of export prices was needed to convert the value forecast into the constant-price terms needed in the analysis of the domestic economy. Export prices are assumed to be affected by changes in home and import costs and by world trade.

Information on *public authorities' current expenditure* comes from estimates published by the government either in the annual White Paper on public expenditure or (since 1968) from the official forecasts of the economy published by the Treasury in the budget-time Financial Statement. *Public fixed investment* comprises investment in dwellings and other investment by both public corporations (broadly, the nationalised industries) and public authorities (both central and local government). Non-dwelling investment is also forecast by the government in the annual public expenditure White Paper. Public sector investment in dwellings can be forecast in broad terms in the light of ministers' announced forward plans, but information on contractors' orders and on dwellings currently under construction can also be used to provide a partially formal relationship between announced programmes of dwellings to be started and actual investment.

Private sector fixed investment is determined partly exogenously. Private investment in dwellings is assumed to be influenced by personal incomes and savings, by the supply of mortgage funds from building societies and

[1] For a fuller informal account of the model see M. J. Artis, 'Short-term economic forecasting at NIESR' in Hilton and Heathfield (eds.), *The Econometric Study of the United Kingdom.*

[2] However, these equations are no longer used (see p. 38).

local authorities, and by the availability of bank credit to builders. There is in addition some direct evidence from builders' reported intentions, but, as with public sector dwelling investment, the forecast is made in a largely informal way and is again essentially an exogenous element. The remainder of the private sector's fixed investment constitutes a more endogenous element in the framework for analysis and forecasting. A very simple lagged accelerator relationship between the level of business investment[1] and past changes in GDP provides a fairly good explanation of the behaviour of investment in the past. Investment by manufacturing industry alone can be explained with considerable precision when it is related to the (calculated) degree of capacity utilisation in the industry, as well as to changes in output. The direct surveys of investment intentions carried out by the government are a further source of information, which may be used to modify, or even supplant, the prediction based on the formal relationships.

Investment in stocks – or stockbuilding – is treated as a wholly endogenous variable. The presumption is that stock-holders wish to maintain a given ratio of stocks to output (a ratio which appears to have declined gradually over the past fifteen years) but that the quarter-to-quarter levels of stockbuilding will be erratic, both because of lags in the adjustment of actual to desired stock levels and because of involuntary changes in stock levels associated with sharp changes in demand and output. The assumption of a relationship between the levels of stock and of output is reasonable: stocks are held principally as a buffer to smooth out short-term dislocations between supply and demand in different parts of the economy. Stocks of raw materials and intermediate goods are held in connection with immediate production, and stocks of finished goods in connection with consumption (by both producers and final consumers). At the most aggregate level, both of these rise in line with total domestic production.

Consumers' expenditure is related, though not in any simple way, to real personal disposable income and to changes in consumer borrowing.[2] Real personal disposable income depends on total personal income, on tax payments and on consumer prices. The main component of personal incomes is the wage and salary bill, forming about 60 per cent of the pre-tax total. The wage and salary bill is the product of average earnings and employment, each of which depends principally, though in different ways, on the pressure of demand.

The rate of change of average earnings depends both on changes in negotiated standard wage rates, and on other factors reflected as changes in wage-drift – that is the tendency for average earnings to rise faster than

[1] That is, investment by the private sector other than in dwellings.

[2] Taken together, personal disposable income and changes in borrowing are sometimes called 'personal disposable funds'.

wage rates. Both negotiated wage rates and wage-drift are influenced by the demand for labour, though with differing emphasis.[1] Changes in wage rates are the outcome of formal negotiations between unions and employers, often at a national level and affecting workers irrespective of region, industry or type of labour. At local level, although earnings are affected by changes in basic or standard negotiated rates, they also reflect circumstances peculiar to the industry, locality, type of firm and so on. These local differences show up through changes in productivity, overtime and profitability. Overall these factors are a stronger influence on wage-drift the higher (and the more rapidly increasing) is the pressure of demand for labour. Wage rates are also influenced by the increase in retail prices – the cost of living.

A substantial amount of empirical work has been done on the determinants of average earnings and wage rates, both at the National Institute and elsewhere, and some of this work is described in more detail in chapter 5. In recent years, however, the operation of the prices and incomes policy has altered the apparent relationships. In particular, the policy has probably had a differential impact on rates and on earnings, affecting negotiated rates the more powerfully, with above average wage-drift tending to mitigate the effect on actual earnings. More debatably, the introduction of the selective employment tax (SET) may have further distorted the normal relationships between average earnings, employment and the wage and salary bill: there is an apparent tendency for employment to be lower and average hours worked by those in employment (and hence average earnings) higher than might otherwise have been expected.

Employment is normally determined by a short-term relationship with output. Actual employment adjusts with a lag to 'desired' employment, which is dependent on the level of output in relation to a productivity trend and to normal hours of work. The trend of growth in productivity is estimated by regression analysis and, in forecasting, extrapolated from recent experience. In this short-term framework, no attempt is made to relate productivity to the rate of capital accumulation.[2]

Total personal income also includes income from self-employment, income from rent and dividends, and net receipts of interest. These are included together as 'other personal income' in the official national income quarterly accounts, though an annual breakdown is available. However, the absence of quarterly figures for these components of personal income has, so far, inhibited a systematic attempt at an empirical investigation of their determinants. Informally, incomes from self-employment seem to

[1] Specifically, the pressure of demand appears to affect wage-drift both more strongly and more immediately than it affects negotiated wage rates.

[2] Partly, of course, because there is no consensus on how such a link could be specified theoretically, but also for the practical reason that, in the short term, such effects on the rate of growth of productivity seem likely to be small.

move in sympathy with the movement in wages and salaries, dividend payments to depend (after a lag) on company profits, and the rent and interest elements to grow in a trend-like way.

Current grants to persons from public authorities are determined primarily exogenously, by government decisions on, for example, benefit rates, but in principle the volume of such transfers also depends on the levels of unemployment and earnings, which are themselves functions of the pressure of demand. The remainder of personal income comprises forces' pay and employers' contributions to National Insurance and private pension funds. Again, these are treated as exogenous elements.

The main deduction to be made from personal income is income tax, which depends on tax rates and the level of incomes. In the aggregate, a distinction is made only between the marginal tax rates on wages and salaries and on other personal income, the latter being significantly higher than the former, largely because this distinction between types of income corresponds roughly with the distinction between earned and unearned income which is reflected in the tax system. Deductions have also to be made for net transfers of cash abroad and for National Insurance and similar contributions by employees, both of which are assumed to be exogenously determined.[1] The resulting aggregate is personal disposable income at current prices.

Consumer prices are assumed to be set on a cost-plus basis, that is by the addition of a fixed profit margin to the average unit costs of production, which comprise labour costs and import costs. Unit labour costs depend on earnings and on productivity; one of the major problems in analysing the behaviour of prices is to decide whether entrepreneurs take actual productivity or the trend in productivity into account in setting prices. Prices are, of course, also affected by changes in indirect tax rates – purchase tax, excise duties, SET and so on. Personal disposable income, adjusted for increases in prices, is referred to as real personal disposable income.

Real personal disposable income is related to consumers' expenditure through the familiar consumption function. Incomes are disaggregated into income from current grants, disposable wages and salaries, and other disposable income, from each of which there are different marginal propensities to save. Current grants, accruing mainly to low-income families, lead to negligible savings; wages and salaries probably have a low, but not zero, savings propensity (empirically, about 8 per cent); while other personal income includes a much larger savings element (of the order of 20 to 25 per cent). Lags also differ: the consumption function is of a simple 'permanent income' type in which permanent income is a function of actual incomes for past periods with geometrically declining weights; the average lag is

[1] National Insurance contributions will in fact be sensitive to changes in unemployment and earnings. As a first approximation, it is assumed that this sensitivity is small enough to be neglected.

longer for other personal income than for wages and salaries or current grants. Special allowance has also to be made for the effect of changes in consumer credit. Such changes are very largely induced by changes in the regulations governing hire purchase transactions and by instructions or guidance given to the banks on personal overdrafts.

The *factor cost adjustment*, the indirect tax content of final expenditure at base-year tax rates, is in fact dependent almost wholly on consumers' expenditure, since by comparison the indirect tax content of other kinds of final expenditure is negligible. Since constant (1963) tax rates are involved, a high degree of explanation is achieved by assuming a constant marginal ratio of factor cost adjustment to consumers' expenditure.

When these various forms of final expenditure – public authorities' current expenditure, fixed investment, exports, consumers' expenditure and stockbuilding – are added up, and the factor cost adjustment is deducted, the result is total final expenditure at factor cost. This is the total demand on resources which must be met either from domestic production or from

Chart 1. *Flow chart of the economy*

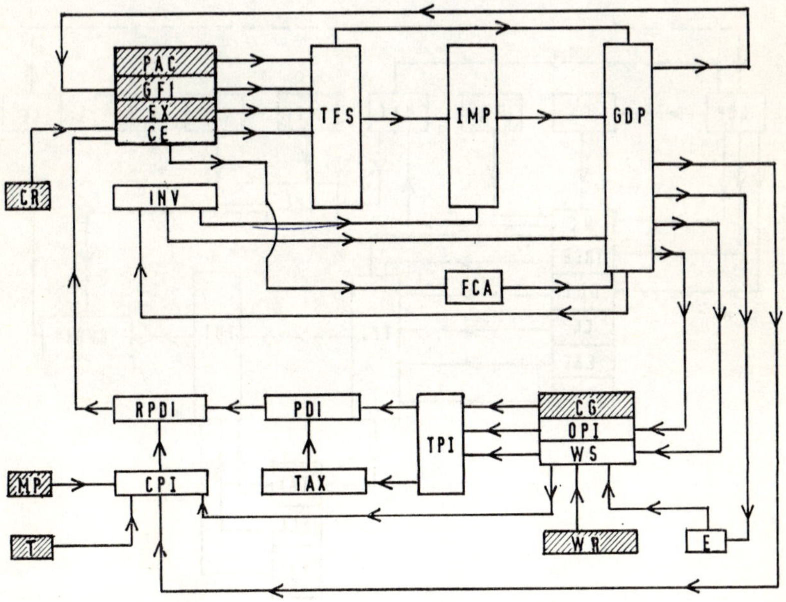

SYMBOLS: see pp. xi, xii. Shaded boxes contain exogenous variables (GFI is partly exogenous).
NOTE: The arrows indicate causal links and not simply quantitative flows.

imports. Since, in practice, it is assumed that the demand for imports is itself given by a simple relationship with total demand, it follows that it is now possible to deduce GDP or total domestic production as, essentially, a residual – that part of the final demand on resources which is not met from imports.

The relationship between total home demand and *imports of goods and services* is a linear one, implying that the marginal propensity to import is constant. A distinction is drawn, however, between stockbuilding and the rest of final expenditure, since the import content of stocks is known to be much higher than the average import content of total final expenditure.

These main connections between the macro-economic quantities are summarised in charts 1 and 2. The first of these shows the main linkages for the economy as a whole, with the complex personal sector shown in an abbreviated form. The second shows the personal sector in more detail. Chart 3 shows the output cycles which the British economy has experienced since 1955.

Chart 2. *Flow chart of the personal sector*

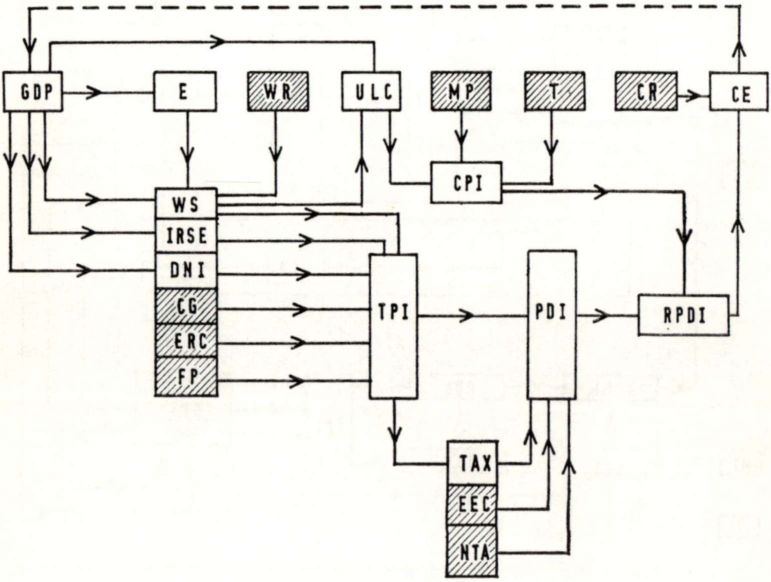

SYMBOLS: see pp. xi, xii. Shaded boxes contain exogenous variables.
NOTE: The arrows indicate causal links and not simply quantitative flows.

Chart 3. *Output growth and output cycles*

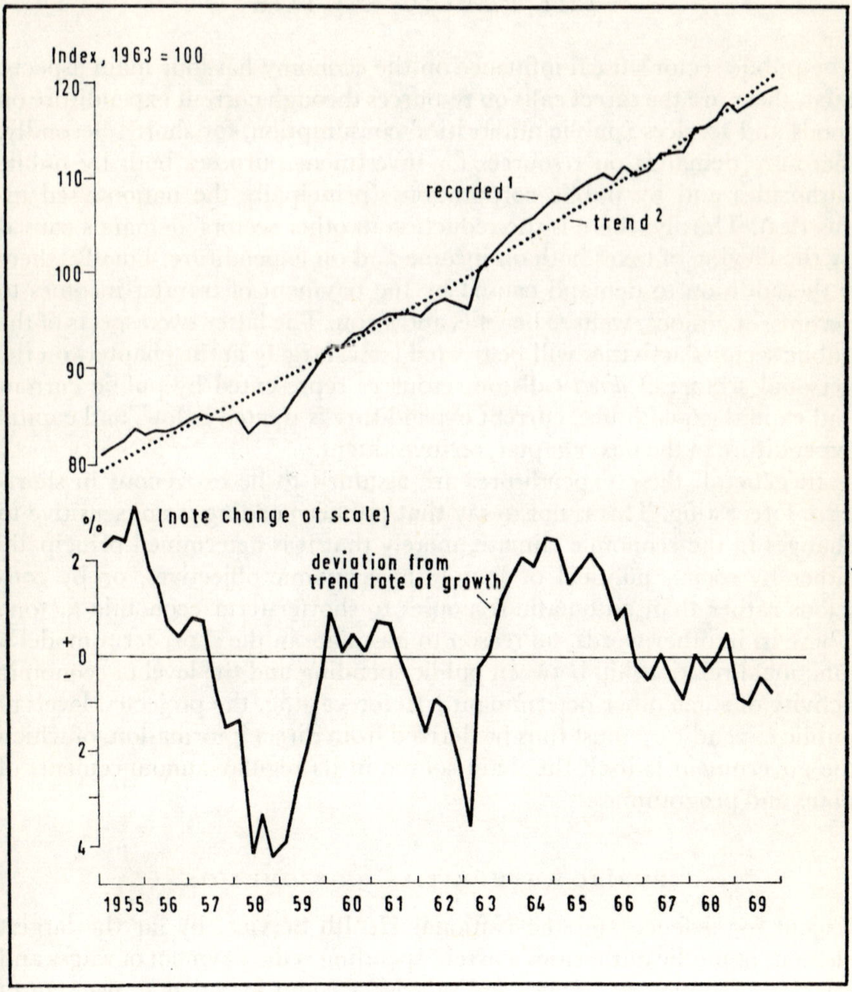

[1] Compromise estimate of GDP (see appendix 1).
[2] Trend rate of growth of GDP = 2·87 per cent per annum compound.

CHAPTER 2

THE PUBLIC SECTOR

The public sector's fiscal influence on the economy has four main aspects. First, there are the direct calls on resources through current expenditure on goods and services (public authorities' consumption, for short). Secondly, there are demands on resources for investment purposes both by public authorities and by public corporations (principally the nationalised industries). Thirdly, there is the reduction in other sectors' demands caused by the levying of taxes both on income and on expenditure. Finally, there is the addition to demand caused by the payment of transfer incomes to persons – pensions, welfare benefits and so on. The latter two aspects of the public sector's activities will be treated later, largely in the chapters on the personal sector; of *direct* calls on resources represented by public current and capital expenditure, current expenditure is treated below, and capital expenditure in the next chapter, on investment.

In general, these expenditures are assumed to be exogenous in short-term forecasting. This is not to say that public spending is not sensitive to changes in the economic climate, merely that it is determined principally either by social, political or long-term economic objectives, or by conscious rather than automatic responses to shorter-term economic factors. There is, in other words, no reason to postulate in the short-term model a functional relationship between public spending and the level of economic activity or some other determinant.[1] In forecasting, the projected levels of public expenditure must thus be derived from direct information, of which the government is itself the main source in its regular announcements of plans and programmes.

PUBLIC AUTHORITIES' CONSUMPTION

Except for defence and the National Health Service, by far the largest element in public authorities' current spending is the payment of wages and salaries to employees. Wages and salaries account for some 55 per cent of total spending, and expenditure on goods for the defence and National Health Service programmes accounts for a further 28 per cent. To a considerable extent, therefore, the problem of predicting the course of current spending reduces to one of predicting the courses of public sector employment and rates of pay.

The principal source for short-term forecasts of public consumption is the

[1] Such links as there are – for example the influence of the levels of unemployment and earnings on National Insurance benefits and contributions – are small in magnitude.

annual White Paper on public expenditure published around the end of the calendar year.[1] The White Paper gives the total of public sector current expenditure at constant prices for the current financial year and for a number of succeeding financial years. The price base is given, for example, as 'at 1969 survey prices', that is the level of prices reckoned to be ruling at the time of the latest public expenditure survey conducted by the government. The translation into 1963 prices, as required by the forecasting framework, is thus not immediately clear; normal practice is to take the rates of increase at constant prices between successive financial years and apply these rates to the base provided by the national accounts statistics. The national accounts do not normally give figures for the whole of the current financial year and thus a certain amount of guess workis involved; fortunately, the previous year's government forecasts of public authorities' consumption are available in the annual Financial Statement. A final problem is the interpolation of the resulting annual totals to arrive at a quarterly forecast, which can only be done by guesswork, assuming smooth quarter-to-quarter movements. Some check on the results is provided by the government's own economic forecasts published at budget time; since the forecast of public authorities' consumption is purely a matter of interpreting official surveys, there is no reason to suppose that there can be a genuine difference of view between official and unofficial forecasters about its future course. Any such divergence is presumed to arise from the greater knowledge of the course of public spending which can be imputed to official forecasters.

There are conceptual problems in measuring public sector demands on real resources. The major difficulty in revaluing public consumption in real terms is that, in general, the final output is not sold to consumers and so no prices can be directly observed. Only in a very limited number of cases – some forms of education, for example – are there competing products provided by private enterprise. In general, it is assumed that changes in numbers employed can be used as indicators of changes in real output, which implies that there is no growth of productivity in the public sector. In some countries, it is assumed that productivity in public services increases at the same rate as in some other industries. The appropriate industries are not easily identified and this approach has been rejected by national accounts statisticians in this country.[2] Nevertheless, the extreme assumption of zero growth of productivity in public services does imply that the revaluation of expenditure projections at constant rates of pay will progressively understate the scale of public consumption, since it ignores the

[1] See, for example, HM Treasury, *Public Expenditure: 1968–69 to 1973–74*, Cmnd 4234, HMSO, 1969.

[2] See *National Accounts Statistics – Sources and Methods*, p. 45; also HM Treasury, *Public Expenditure: a new presentation*, Cmnd 4017, HMSO, 1969, pp. 22–4, and *Public Expenditure: 1968–69 to 1973–74*, pp. 77–9.

fact that advances in technology and organisation enable the same number of soldiers, policemen, doctors and teachers to 'produce' more and more over time.[1] The short-term forecaster must comfort himself with the thought that differences in the rates of growth of productivity in the public and private sectors are likely to be much the same in the immediate future as in the past few years, and that the trend of this difference will be reflected in a biased estimate of the productivity trend in his production or employment function for the economy as a whole.

[1] Accordingly, allowance is now madei n official projections of government expenditure as a whole for a 'relative price effect', but hitherto there has been no breakdown of the kind needed in analysis and forecasting (see *Public Expenditure: a new presentation*, pp. 22–4).

CHAPTER 3

INVESTMENT

FIXED INVESTMENT

Gross domestic fixed capital formation – fixed investment for short – represents producers' purchases of buildings, machinery, vehicles or plant which will give services to production over a number of years. For purposes of analysis and forecasting, it is necessary to distinguish between different kinds of fixed investment both by sector and industry and by type of investment, since the economic forces at work in these categories are quite distinct. The breakdown used is:

Public sector

public authorities' non-dwelling investment
public corporations' investment
public sector investment in dwellings

Private sector

manufacturing industry's investment
other private industry's investment[1]
private sector investment in dwellings

In addition, within the private sector, a distinction can be drawn between industry's investment in vehicles, plant and machinery and in buildings.

Public sector non-dwelling investment is treated as being determined wholly exogenously both for the past and in forecasting. This simply reflects the fact that public expenditure decisions (including investment) are made on complex social and political as well as economic grounds. Indeed, economic considerations operate more by modifying the other factors than by directly affecting the level of expenditure. In other words, the prospect of a medium-term imbalance between supply and demand in the economy may cause the government to trim its existing plans for public investment but cannot be said to determine its future level directly.

Fortunately, from the point of view of forecasting demand, the government publishes a certain amount of information about its future investment plans.[2] As with public consumption (see chapter 2 above), forward projections are given at constant survey prices, and problems arise in translating them into 1963 prices and interpolating the financial year totals to give a quarterly forecast.

[1] 'Other private industry' includes construction, transport (including shipping), agriculture, mining, distribution and some other service industries.

[2] See for example, *Public Expenditure 1968–69 to 1973–74*, especially table 3.5, p. 69.

A full account of the methods of forecasting *public sector housing investment* was given by Nobay.[1] As in the case of other public investment, the size of the public sector housing programme is essentially a government decision. Forward plans announced from time to time by ministers provide estimates of the likely rate of starts on new dwellings. But the connection between starts and investment is complex: factors of which account has to be taken include the rate of quality improvement, the proportion of high-rise dwellings (blocks of flats), and variation in the time taken from start to completion. Statistics are available of the number of dwellings under construction, and a relationship between investment, number of starts, number of dwellings under construction and the average construction period has been estimated:

$$(3.1)\quad \log_{10}I = 0{\cdot}0034 + \underset{(0{\cdot}004)}{0{\cdot}4171}\log_{10}S + \underset{(0{\cdot}068)}{0{\cdot}5586}\log_{10}UC - \underset{(0{\cdot}128)}{1{\cdot}3593}CT$$

$$R^2 = 0{\cdot}58 \qquad DW = 2{\cdot}36$$

where I = public investment in dwellings in £ thousand millions at 1958 prices,
S = number of starts,
UC = number of dwellings under construction
and CT = average construction period,
all seasonally adjusted and in the same quarter.

But this relationship does not provide a very high degree of explanation, only 58 per cent of the variation being accounted for. The influence of unquantifiable factors – quality, the high-rise proportion and so on – remains important and the forecast is normally made in a relatively informal way.

The relation between starts and investment seems to be rather stronger in *private sector housing*. One equation relates the change in investment in a given quarter to changes in starts in the current and in previous quarters:

$$(3.2)\quad \log_{10}(I/I_{-1}) = 0{\cdot}0033 + \underset{(0{\cdot}004)}{0{\cdot}43}\log_{10}(S/S_{-1}) + \underset{(0{\cdot}004)}{0{\cdot}14}\log_{10}(S_{-1}/S_{-2}) + \underset{(0{\cdot}004)}{0{\cdot}19}\log_{10}(S_{-2}/S_{-3}) + \underset{(0{\cdot}004)}{0{\cdot}06}\log_{10}(S_{-3}/S_{-4})$$

$$R^2 = 0{\cdot}78 \qquad DW = 2{\cdot}44$$

where I = private investment in dwellings in £ thousand millions at 1958 prices
and S = number of starts,
both seasonally adjusted.

The problem remains of explaining and predicting the level of starts in the

[1] A. R. Nobay, 'Short-term forecasting of housing investment', *National Institute Economic Review*, No. 41, August 1967.

private sector. Influences on the demand side likely to be most important are the levels of personal incomes and savings and the expected supply of mortgage advances. On the supply side, an important consideration is that the bulk of private housing is speculatively built rather than built to order, so that builders are heavily dependent on the availability of bank credit; the stock of unsold houses is also an important factor. Some information is available directly from the building industry's own surveys of forward intentions. Little progress has, however, been made in treating these influences econometrically;[1] the forecast of private sector starts is therefore made informally.

The remainder of fixed investment – *private non-dwelling investment* – comes closest to the familiar textbook macro-economic concept of investment. In very general terms, the desire to invest depends on the evolution of demand in relation to the growth of supply capacity. In principle, the rate of interest may, by affecting the cost of financing capital expansion and hence the profitability of investment, modify the basic relationship; as may also government policy in respect of investment incentives or grants.

Very broadly, one can distinguish four main types of investment theory, according to whether investment is held to depend on the rate of change of output (accelerator theories), on the level of capacity utilisation, on financial variables (principally profits) or on marginal considerations of the kind familiar in neo-classical analyses. In practice, it turns out to be very difficult to distinguish empirically between the first three kinds of explanation, while little empirical work on the fourth hypothesis has yet been done at the National Institute. The length of the lag between a change in the determining factors and the consequential change in investment is unknown. Although changes in output, the level of capacity utilisation and the level of profits are not simultaneously correlated, there can be a very high degree of correlation between them when different lags are taken into account.

The simplest kind of accelerator theory suggests that if output grows at a constant rate, *net* investment will proceed at a constant level. In fact, the statistics, which relate to *gross* investment, show a substantial upward trend. This may be explained to some extent by replacement investment, but it also strongly suggests an upward trend in the desired capital–output ratio.[2]

[1] See Nobay, 'Short-term forecasting of housing investment' *loc. cit.* for a fuller account.

[2] In the simplest case, let the desired capital – output ratio, $K^*/Y = a + bt$.
Then $K^* = aY + btY$ and desired net investment, I^*, is

$$\frac{dK^*}{dt} = a\frac{dY}{dt} + bt\frac{dY}{dt} + bY.$$

If output grows steadily, say $Y = g + ht$, then

$$\begin{aligned} I^* &= ah + bht + bg + bht \\ &= a' + b't. \end{aligned}$$

A similar time dependency will be introduced if, as a first approximation, replacement investment is taken to grow over time with the growth of capital stock.

A simple way of estimating such a relationship is to take deviations from trends in both investment and output, and to regress the former on changes in the latter. The (logarithmic) trends estimated by ordinary least squares over the period 1958–67 were:

$$(3.3)\quad \begin{aligned} \log_e \text{PNDI} &= 6{\cdot}35 + 0{\cdot}01247t \\ \log_e \text{GDP} &= 8{\cdot}80 + 0{\cdot}007996t \end{aligned}$$

where PNDI = private gross non-dwelling investment in £ millions at 1963 prices
and t = 0 in 1958 I.

These trend rates of growth are 5·0 per cent per annum for private investment and 3·1 per cent per annum for GDP.[1]

Deviations from the logarithmic trend in private non-dwelling investment were then regressed on a set of lagged changes in the corresponding GDP deviations, with the following results for the most satisfactory set:

$$(3.4)\quad \begin{aligned} \text{DP} &= \underset{(0{\cdot}50)}{1{\cdot}41\Delta \text{DG}_{-3}} + \underset{(0{\cdot}50)}{1{\cdot}83\Delta \text{DG}_{-4}} + \underset{(0{\cdot}51)}{1{\cdot}78\Delta \text{DG}_{-5}} \\ &\quad + \underset{(0{\cdot}51)}{2{\cdot}56\Delta \text{DG}_{-6}} + \underset{(0{\cdot}46)}{1{\cdot}19\Delta \text{DG}_{-7}} + \underset{(0{\cdot}46)}{0{\cdot}59\Delta \text{DG}_{-8}} \\ \text{SE} &= 2{\cdot}43\,\% \end{aligned}$$

where DP = deviation of $\log_e$ PNDI from trend
and Δ DG = change in deviation of $\log_e$GDP from trend.

When this equation is rearranged to include the time-trends in output and investment it becomes:

$$(3.5)\quad \begin{aligned} \log_e \text{PNDI} = {} & 6{\cdot}275 + 1{\cdot}41\Delta\log_e \text{GDP}_{-3} \\ & + 1{\cdot}83\Delta\log_e \text{GDP}_{-4} + 1{\cdot}78\Delta\log_e \text{GDP}_{-5} \\ & + 2{\cdot}56\Delta\log_e \text{GDP}_{-6} + 1{\cdot}19\Delta\log_e \text{GDP}_{-7} \\ & + 0{\cdot}59\Delta\log_e \text{GDP}_{-8} + 0{\cdot}01247t \end{aligned}$$

where $\Delta\log_e \text{GDP}_{-i}$ = change in $\log_e$ GDP in that quarter
and the other variables are as defined for equation 3·3.

The mean lag implied by this relationship is between five and six quarters, and the implicit marginal capital–output ratio (with output measured annually) is 0·24.

More sophisticated investigations have been carried out into the behaviour of investment by manufacturing industry.[2] In this case, a distinction is drawn between the factors determining the changes in the desired

[1] In this, and subsequent empirical work, the investment figures were adjusted to take account of the exogenously induced boom in steel investment in 1961.

[2] A. R. Nobay, 'Forecasting manufacturing investment – some preliminary results', *National Institute Economic Review*, No. 52, May 1970.

capital stock and the factors affecting the institutional steps through which the desired change is realised – planning, ordering and the gestation period. In practice, investment expenditures are directly determined by appropriations or orders for investment goods; it is appropriations rather than investment itself which are directly linked to changes in the desired capital stock.

In specifying the determinants of the level of appropriations, it is assumed that, for given capital–output ratios, manufacturers appropriate funds for investment in order to maintain a specific target level of (capital) capacity utilisation. This optimum level of capacity utilisation is assumed to be relatively stable, determined by minimum cost considerations. Because of the time lags involved in the ordering and delivering of capital goods, it is assumed that, in a given period, manufacturers appropriate both to correct the discrepancy between the existing and optimum levels of utilisation, and to maintain the optimum level of utilisation for some time ahead. This latter time is given by the lag between orders and deliveries of capital equipment. Appropriations will thus depend principally on the current level of capacity utilisation, and on expectations about the future rate of growth of output and hence of desired capacity.

The relationship between appropriations and actual investment is mainly determined by the lag between orders and deliveries, which will probably vary over the investment cycle, largely because of supply limitations in the capital goods industries.

For the United Kingdom no data on manufacturers' appropriations are available, and so the theoretical structure outlined above has to be compressed into one relationship between investment and the other variables – capacity utilisation, expected output changes, financial variables and supply limitations in the capital goods industry. The time lag between appropriations and investment is estimated directly from available data for orders on hand, net new orders and deliveries. On the assumption of 'first in, first out' in satisfying orders, the lag for engineering goods appears to vary from 3·3 to 3·9 quarters, including both construction and waiting periods. A detailed industry-by-industry analysis for orders placed in the first quarter of 1965 suggests that, on average, the waiting time is nearly three times as long as the production time, but that there is considerable variation between the different industries. For the purpose of the empirical investigations, a four-quarter period was taken as the lag between orders and deliveries, and a further quarter as the planning period which elapses between changes in the variables governing the decision to invest and the placing of firm orders. The total lag of five quarters agrees with that found in the simple accelerator model described earlier.

In the econometric work, the measure used for capacity is based on the ratio of the series for seasonally adjusted manufacturing output to its trend value. The largest positive value is taken as the full-capacity level, and deviations of the ratio from this level as the degree of under-utilisation of capacity. The expected change in output is taken as the actual output change between the decision and the investment five quarters later. Supply constraints in the capital goods sector are represented by the waiting time involved. Investment allowances and grants payable by the government are allowed for by using a variable to represent the net cost of £1,000 invested. This is calculated by deducting the present value of tax savings from £1,000 and using the medium-term government security yield as the interest rate to give the net cost of financing the remainder. A representative result is:

$$\text{(3.6)} \quad MI = -479 + \underset{(10{\cdot}8)^*}{5{\cdot}35 CAP_{-5}} + \underset{(10{\cdot}3)^*}{2{\cdot}76 \Delta O} - \underset{(3{\cdot}2)^*}{15{\cdot}93 PT_{-4}} + \underset{(15{\cdot}6)^*}{1{\cdot}20t}$$

$$R^2 = 0{\cdot}96 \qquad DW = 1{\cdot}41$$

where MI = manufacturing investment excluding steel and chemicals,
CAP = capacity utilisation,
ΔO = change in output between current quarter and $t-5$,
PT = capital goods production time
and $t = 0$ in 1959 I,
all quarterly, in £ millions at 1958 prices where appropriate, and seasonally adjusted.
(* The bracketed figures are *t*-ratios.)

Other regressions showed that the cost-of-capital variable had virtually no effect on the degree of explanation and that the introduction of profits variables also failed to improve the explanation.

Taken together, these empirical results illustrate three main points about the behaviour of private sector investment. First, it makes little difference whether capacity utilisation, the change in output or the level of profits is taken as the main explanatory variable, simply because these three have varied so closely together in the post-war British economy. Secondly, the average lag between a variation in output growth (or capacity utilisation, or profits) and the induced change in investment is fairly firmly established at about five quarters. Thirdly, the effect of changes in the cost of investment, whether induced by changes in investment incentives or by changes in interest rates, seems to be very small indeed.

A separate means of forecasting private industry's investment is through the direct surveys of investment intentions carried out by the Department of Trade and Industry (formerly the Board of Trade and, for manufacturing industry, the Ministry of Technology).[1] The results are given separately for manufacturing industry, for shipping, and for distributive and

[1] Supplementary data on intentions and business opinion are provided by the periodical surveys conducted by the Confederation of British Industry and the *Financial Times*.

service industries. These surveys are conducted three times a year; until very recently the actual information provided by the sample of firms was not published, but only the official interpretation of the survey data. It seems likely that the relationship between reported investment intentions and actual investment will vary over time and over the business cycle. Now that the survey data are available, it should be possible to connect the relationship between industry's forecast and the out-turn with other variables, such as the pressure of demand. Formerly, we had to take on trust the official interpretation of the survey.

This information is set alongside the results of the econometric relationships used in forecasting private investment. There is, of course, no formal way in which any conflict between the two forecasts can be resolved; on the one hand, information provided directly by firms may be excessively volatile in response to small changes in the economic outlook, but, on the other hand, the more stable econometric relationships estimated over past years may not take account of special factors affecting the outlook of which entrepreneurs will have been able to take note. The forecast is likely to represent a compromise between the two methods, with the investment intentions survey receiving greater weight the more distinctive the current economic situation is compared with past experience.[1]

STOCKBUILDING

Investment in stocks, or stockbuilding, has varied very markedly. It appears that the periods of very high stockbuilding have coincided with, or immediately followed, the output peaks of 1955, 1960 and 1964, while periods of low stockbuilding were associated with the recessions of 1958, 1962 and 1966–7. What is not clear is whether these variations served merely to maintain the level of stocks in relation to the volume of output, or whether the stock–output ratio has itself fluctuated over time. There seems to have been a secular decline in the ratio to quarterly GDP from about 1·8 in the 1950s to little more than 1·5 recently. There have also been cyclical variations: broadly speaking, periods of rapid rise in output (in 1955, 1959–60 and 1963–4) have been associated with low levels of the stock–output ratio relative to the trend value, while periods of slow growth (1957–8, 1960–1 and, less clearly, 1966–7) have been associated with high stock–output ratios.

One plausible explanation of these phenomena is that the equilibrium (or desired) ratio of stocks to output has followed a smooth trend, but the rate of stockbuilding required to preserve this equilibrium as output changes has been adjusted only slowly. Thus, in a given quarter the level of stocks

[1] This dilemma also arises in connection with simulation studies of the past (see below, chapter 8).

will lag behind the equilibrium level associated with the current level of output, with the result that a rise in GDP is initially associated with a *fall* in the stock–output ratio, followed by a recovery as stockbuilding increases.

Algebraically, suppose that the desired stock–output ratio follows a smooth trend:

$$S^*/GDP = \alpha + \beta t$$

where S^* = desired level of stocks,
and t = time-trend.

And suppose that the adjustment in one quarter is a constant proportion, λ, of the gap between the desired level of stocks and the actual level, S, ruling at the beginning of the quarter:

$$S - S_{-1} = \lambda(S^* - S_{-1}),$$

then

$$S = (1 - \lambda)S_{-1} + \alpha\lambda GDP + \beta\lambda t GDP.$$

Regression analysis (with stocks and GDP in £ millions) gives:

$$(3.7) \quad S = \underset{(0.035)}{0.798}S_{-1} + \underset{(0.054)}{0.314}GDP - \underset{(0.00019)}{0.00119}tGDP$$

$$R^2 = 0.999 \qquad SE = 48.3 \qquad DW = 1.59$$

From 3.7, values for the structural parameters can be calculated. They are:

$$\alpha = 1.55 \qquad \beta = -0.0059 \qquad \lambda = 0.202$$

In view of the substantial serial correlation present in the errors, this relationship was re-estimated in first difference form, giving:

$$(3.8) \quad \Delta S = \underset{(0.120)}{0.482}\Delta S_{-1} + \underset{(0.101)}{0.329}\Delta GDP + \underset{(0.00201)}{0.00263}\Delta(tGDP)$$

$$R^2 = 0.648 \qquad SE = 57.6 \qquad DW = 2.55$$

The implicit structural parameters are:

$$\alpha = 0.64 \qquad \beta = 0.0051 \qquad \lambda = 0.518$$

These values are very different from those based on equation 3.7; furthermore, the time-trend term has reversed sign and become insignificant, while the degree of explanation is lower.

One factor omitted in equation 3.7 is the influence of involuntary changes in stockbuilding caused by unexpected changes in final demand. To test for this, we can include the change in total final sales as a factor:[1]

$$S - S_{-1} = \lambda(S^* - S_{-1}) - \gamma\Delta TFS$$

[1] Strictly it should be the *unexpected* part of the change in total final sales.

On estimation, this gives:

$$(3.9)\quad S = \underset{(0{\cdot}036)}{0{\cdot}773}S_{-1} + \underset{(0{\cdot}054)}{0{\cdot}354}GDP - \underset{(0{\cdot}0002)}{0{\cdot}0013}tGDP - \underset{(0{\cdot}058)}{0{\cdot}134}\Delta TFS$$

$$R^2 = 0{\cdot}999 \qquad SE = 46{\cdot}4 \qquad DW = 1{\cdot}46$$

or, when a constant term is included:

$$(3.10)\quad S = \underset{(352)}{-779} + \underset{(0{\cdot}039)}{0{\cdot}814}S_{-1} + \underset{(0{\cdot}054)}{0{\cdot}380}GDP - \underset{(0{\cdot}0005)}{0{\cdot}0023}tGDP - \underset{(0{\cdot}056)}{0{\cdot}136}\Delta TFS$$

$$R^2 = 0{\cdot}999 \qquad SE = 44{\cdot}8 \qquad DW = 1{\cdot}65$$

The implied structural parameters are:

For 3.9: $\alpha = 1{\cdot}56 \quad \beta = -0{\cdot}0088 \quad \lambda = 0{\cdot}227$
For 3.10: $\alpha = 2{\cdot}04 \quad \beta = -0{\cdot}0126 \quad \lambda = 0{\cdot}186$

Both sets are plausible, and there is little to choose between these two equations in terms of goodness of fit. In view of the difficulty of justifying theoretically the inclusion of a constant term, equation 3.9 is probably the more satisfactory. Nevertheless, it explains only a little over half of the total variation in stockbuilding, which thus remains the element in the analysis probably least satisfactorily explained.[1]

Clearly, a good deal of further research could usefully be devoted to the behaviour of stocks. In particular, the influence of monetary factors and the usefulness of disaggregation could be investigated, although some preliminary work on these aspects has not seemed immediately promising. One important inhibiting factor in the empirical analysis is the relatively poor quality of the statistics; the Central Statistical Office itself points out that in addition to other problems there is 'a major uncertainty ... on the validity of the basic assumptions about the nature of the accounting valuations'.[2]

[1] There is also a presumption that the specification and method of estimation of these models need examining further. This is indicated by the variability of the estimates of the parameters.

[2] *National Accounts Statistics – Sources and Methods*, p. 407.

CHAPTER 4

FOREIGN TRADE

EXPORTS OF GOODS

Exports are regarded as being determined principally exogenously;[1] specifically, they are supposed to be influenced only to a small extent by changing circumstances within the home economy. The influence on the supply of exports of varying pressure of demand at home, and also of changes in competitiveness reflected in the relationship between British export prices and those of other countries, may have some small effect. Bu the level of exports, at least in the short-run, is thought of as depending mainly on the situation prevailing in the world outside the British economy

In general, the forecasting of exports is done subjectively or informally The main factors influencing the forecast are the likely rates of economi growth of the industrial countries, and the current and prospective foreig exchange positions of the less developed countries. But the weights to b attached to these factors are not determined in any very precise or system atic way, and account is additionally taken, in an *ad hoc* fashion, of report of individual large export orders, of forecasts made by industry spokesme and, formerly, of responses to the National Institute's annual Industria Inquiry (now discontinued), in addition to any other special consideration arising from time to time.[2]

While we seem up to now to forecast better by informal means than b econometric methods, the main factors taken into account are similar both cases. The description below of our econometric work may therefor be of interest, even though the results have not on the whole proved reliab beyond the estimation period.

Since about the beginning of the 1960s imports into most of the industri countries have been very largely free to vary with the general level demand, and it is reasonable to search for links between imports an demand indicators. In primary producing countries the situation is mo complex: their imports are often subject to control and there is more like to be a link with export earnings, aid receipts and changes in the levels reserves. Further, the United Kingdom share of imports of manufactures in sterling area countries (almost entirely primary producers) has fallen muc faster than its share of imports of manufactures into industrial countrie

[1] In this chapter 'exports' means exports of goods only. Exports of services are dealt with the section on the balance of payments at the end of chapter 9.

[2] See R. L. Major ,'Forecasting exports and imports: Introduction', *National Institute Econo Review*, No. 42, November 1967.

[3] The problem of forecasting world trading conditions is discussed further in chapter 9 belo

EXPORTS OF MANUFACTURES TO INDUSTRIAL COUNTRIES

A method of forecasting British exports of manufactures to industrial countries has been described.[1] Two basic assumptions were made: that the movement of total demand in industrial countries was the principal determinant of their imports of manufactures, and that the movement of these imports was the main determinant of the British share.

Imports of manufactures can be expected to move more closely with home demand for manufactures than with home demand for all goods and services; this prompted the use of the volume index of manufacturing output as the relevant indicator of industrial countries' demand. The weighted index was then related to the total volume of the intra-trade between the industrial countries. Allowance had to be made for gradual trade liberalisation, the effect of which has been to produce a trend-like rise in the ratio of intra-trade to production. The best empirical relationship seemed to be:[2]

$$(4.1)\quad Z = 4{\cdot}01 + \underset{(0{\cdot}18)}{1{\cdot}355P_m} - \underset{(0{\cdot}60)}{1{\cdot}511(\rho/\pi)_{-1}} + \underset{(0{\cdot}001)}{0{\cdot}002t}$$

$$R^2 = 0{\cdot}997 \qquad DW = 0{\cdot}53$$

where Z = value of industrial countries' imports of manufactures in \$ millions,

P_m = weighted index of industrial countries' manufacturing production,

ρ = weighted index of export prices,

π = weighted index of wholesale prices of manufactures

and t = 0 in 1961 II,

all quarterly, seasonally adjusted and in logarithms base 10.

The value of intra-trade was made to depend on the volume of production, relative home and export prices, and a time-trend. In many ways, this relationship is unsatisfactory: it relates the *value* of trade to the *volume* of production, the price statistics are unreliable (especially for exports, where average value indices, which can change with the pattern of trade, are often used) and the export price series takes no account of differential changes in tariffs. Nevertheless, the relationship fitted well over the estimation period, and attempts to improve it did not succeed. Attempts to introduce a cyclical element representing the net effect of changes in the pressure of demand, and to introduce a system of lags, have failed; the statistical problems associated with the price series are probably insoluble.

The second stage was to examine the relationship between British exports and industrial countries' imports of manufactures. The two are highly

[1] G. A. Renton, 'Forecasting British exports of manufactures to industrial countries', *National Institute Economic Review*, No. 42, November 1967. The estimation period was 1956–66.

[2] Renton, *loc. cit.*, p. 39.

correlated, but the British share has fallen at a varying rate. Changes in the area and commodity composition of trade contribute very little to the explanation of the fall in share.[1] Lack of competitiveness in general may be a factor, but the inclusion of a relative price variable in the regression analysis gave perverse results – suggesting that a rise in the price of British exports relative to competing goods leads to a rise in the volume of British exports.[2] The pressure of demand in the British economy did, however, appear to have a measurable impact on the level of exports. It is to be expected that if, as is commonly claimed, home sales are more profitable than export sales, then preference will tend to be given to the home market, but when demand pressure is low at home the cost of maintaining spare capacity will outweigh the extra cost of exporting. Exports should thus be negatively correlated with the home pressure of demand, at any rate in the short term. (It has been argued that in the longer term, a high pressure of demand leads to higher investment and faster technological change, thus assisting exports.) When the value of exports of manufactures was related to industrial intra-trade, home demand pressure and a time-trend, the following result was obtained:

$$(4.2)\quad X = -0{\cdot}9579 + \underset{(0{\cdot}094)}{1{\cdot}0213Z} - \underset{(0{\cdot}163)}{0{\cdot}7734Q_{-1}} - \underset{(0{\cdot}001)}{0{\cdot}0034t}$$

$$R^2 = 0{\cdot}996 \qquad DW = 1{\cdot}77$$

where X = value of United Kingdom exports of manufactures to industrial countries in $ millions,

Q = ratio of United Kingdom manufacturing production to trend

and other variables were as defined for equation 4.1, all quarterly, seasonally adjusted and in logarithms base 10.

The implications of equations 4.1 and 4.2 were as follows: a rise in the volume of industrial countries' manufacturing production of 1 per cent would raise the value of their intra-trade in manufactured goods by 1·36 per cent; a rise in this intra-trade by 1 per cent would raise British exports by 1·02 per cent. Other things being equal, the industrial countries' intra-trade would grow some 2 per cent a year faster than their rate of growth of production, while Britain's share would fall by some 3 per cent a year. Variations in the home pressure of demand of the magnitude which have been seen since 1955 might affect exports by up to 3 per cent in any year.

EXPORTS TO PRIMARY PRODUCING COUNTRIES

It has already been remarked that the factors determining primary producers' imports are likely to differ from those governing industrial countries'

[1] See *National Institute Economic Review*, No. 39, February 1967, p. 16, table 6.
[2] Renton, *loc. cit.*, p. 42, table 2.

imports. The primary producers are assumed to have a permanent excess demand for imports from the industrial countries and the level of actual imports is held to be determined by the constraints imposed by the funds available – receipts from exports, and from aid and foreign investment. Of these determinants, export receipts are likely to be the most important and the sub-model for explaining British exports thus has three elements: the explanation of primary producers' exports, the explanation of primary producers' imports and the explanation of the British share of these imports.

Primary producers' exports to the industrial countries are highly dependent on OECD manufacturing production and on export prices. One relationship which gave a good explanation in the estimation period was:[1]

$$(4.3)\quad Z = \underset{(0{\cdot}50)}{0{\cdot}462} + \underset{(0{\cdot}17)}{0{\cdot}394}P + \underset{(0{\cdot}14)}{1{\cdot}344}p + \underset{(0{\cdot}0025)}{0{\cdot}0085}t + \text{seasonals}$$

$R^2 = 0{\cdot}989 \qquad DW = 1{\cdot}56$

where Z = primary producers' exports to industrial countries in $ millions,

P = index of industrial countries' manufacturing production,

p = index of primary producers' export prices

and t = 0 in 1954 IV.

Seasonal dummies (not shown) were used to estimate seasonality, and all variables were in logarithms base e.

The relationship between export receipts and imports is complex; there is no reason to postulate an immediate and automatic adjustment of import demand to export receipts. Without going into the specification of a plausible mechanism, the dependence of primary producers' imports on their exports and on their gold and foreign exchange reserves was demonstrated empirically:

$$(4.4)\quad M = \underset{(0{\cdot}285)}{0{\cdot}977} + \underset{(0{\cdot}047)}{0{\cdot}821}Z_{-2} + \underset{(0{\cdot}087)}{0{\cdot}260}R_{-2} + \text{seasonals}$$

$R^2 = 0{\cdot}967 \qquad DW = 1{\cdot}32$

where M = industrial countries' exports to primary producers in $ millions,

R = primary producers' gold and foreign exchange reserves in $ thousand millions

and other variables were as defined for equation 4.3, all quarterly and in logarithms base e.

Finally, the share of United Kingdom exports in primary producers'

[1] For a fuller exposition see A. H. C. Broadbent, E. A. Anyanwu and N. Garganas, 'Forecasting trade between OECD countries and primary producers', *National Institute Economic Review*, No. 52, May 1970. The estimation period was 1955–67.

total imports from industrial countries was simply explained in terms of the ratio of United Kingdom to OECD export prices and a time-trend:

$$(4.5)\quad s = \underset{(2{\cdot}70)}{6{\cdot}92} - \underset{(0{\cdot}583)}{1{\cdot}832}r_{-4} - \underset{(0{\cdot}0016)}{0{\cdot}0042}t + \text{seasonals}$$

$$R^2 = 0{\cdot}941 \qquad DW = 1{\cdot}80$$

where s = ratio of United Kingdom to total OECD exports to primary producers,

r = ratio of United Kingdom to total OECD export prices

and $t = 0$ in 1958 IV,

with all variables quarterly and in logarithms base e.

OTHER EXPORTS

Exports to primary producers and exports of manufactures to industrial countries together account for some 85 per cent of total British exports of goods. There has as yet been no successful attempt to provide a formal framework of analysis for the remaining 15 per cent – exports of non-manufactures to industrial countries, and exports to countries other than primary producers and industrial countries.[1] For forecasting purposes, informal projections are made for these categories.

TOTAL EXPORTS OF GOODS

An attempt has been made to develop a forecasting relationship for the aggregate value of exports of goods, both because the relationships described above do not cover all exports of goods, and because no one equation or set of equations is ever entirely satisfactory in the context of economic forecasting.

Several indicators of demand for exports have been tested in the aggregate relationship, including world industrial production and real gross national product (GNP) of the industrial countries. However, the most satisfactory indicator was found to be the index of industrial countries' manufacturing production, as used in the relationship for exports of manufactures described above.[2] Other factors tested in the aggregate relationship were the levels of primary producers' reserves and of their export prices, the pressure of demand in the United Kingdom (measured either by unemployment or by the ratio of manufacturing production to trend) and the prices of British exports relative to those of major competitors. None of these, however, were statistically significant. The only other variable included in

[1] I.e. Finland, Greece, Spain, Turkey and the Communist countries.

[2] See pp. 39–40.

the equation, in addition to the index of industrial countries' manufacturing production, was the ratio of the latter to its trend: this appeared with a negative sign, presumably indicating that any pressure of (foreign) demand effect – which would suggest a positive coefficient – is outweighed by the tendency already noted for the British share of world trade in manufactures to fall faster the greater the rate of growth of total trade.

The resulting relationship produced highly autocorrelated residuals, whose pattern when estimated was found to be highly significant and in the form of a second-order difference equation.[1] From one point of view the relationship is thus unsatisfactory: it is of little value – and perhaps rather dangerous – to use a relationship in forecasting which produces a cyclical pattern of residuals around the central projection when there is no hypothesis as to the cause of such a cycle.[2] On the other hand, the making of proper allowance for serial correlation in this way means that the estimates of the other parameters in the equation should be statistically more efficient. In forecasting, the relationship is used to make a central forecast; autocorrelation is ignored for the future.

The estimates are:

$$\log_e X = \underset{(18\cdot4)}{2\cdot7932} + \underset{(26\cdot8)}{0\cdot817} \log_e P - \underset{(2\cdot18)}{0\cdot173} \log_e P/T + u \qquad (4.6)$$

where $u = \underset{(6\cdot1)}{0\cdot861} u_{-1} - \underset{(2\cdot1)}{0\cdot289} u_{-2}$

and X = value of United Kingdom exports of goods in £ millions,
P = index of industrial countries' manufacturing production,
$\log_e P/T$ = ratio of $\log_e P$ to its linear trend.

IMPORTS

Imports are a major element in both the model of the domestic economy and in the framework for analysing the balance of payments. In terms of the domestic economy, the volume of imports of goods and services represents the portion of final demand which is not met from home production; the volume of imports is thus principally determined by the level of home demand. This volume of imports is then taken as an exogenous element in the balance of payments framework. In general, the principal import relationships which have been investigated have been aggregative, making no distinction between different categories of imports – foodstuffs, raw materials, manufactures, and so on – though some work has been done on more disaggregated lines.

Aggregate import relationships have been described by Godley and

[1] Thus generating a cyclical pattern of errors in the original equation.
[2] The period of oscillation of this cycle would be about ten quarters.

Shepherd[1] and re-examined by Black, Kidgell and Ray.[2] The basic hypotheses used in these analyses were that imports would be related to the total level of demand for goods and services in the economy, that they would vary with the composition of demand, since different kinds of demand have different marginal import contents, and that the overall pressure of demand would be significant, since at high pressures of demand marginal import propensities are likely to rise as home supply becomes inadequate. Relative prices of imports compared with domestically produced substitutes ought also to be an influence.

Table 2. *Import propensities in categories of domestic demand*[a]

Percentages

	Average import propensities		Implied marginal propensity,
	1954	1963	1954–63
Consumer's expenditure	16·4	17·0	19
Public authorities' current expenditure	6·1	8·8	67
Gross fixed investment	10·1	14·3	22
Exports	17·1	22·9	40
Total final sales	14·0	16·4	25

SOURCES: Central Statistical Office, *Input–Output Tables for the United Kingdom, No. 8, 1954* and *No. 16, 1963*, HMSO, 1961 and 1970.

[a] At 1963 prices.

The importance of distinguishing between different categories of domestic demand is illustrated by the average import propensities revealed by the official input–output tables for 1954 and 1963 and shown in table 2. There is clearly some difference – though not a very marked one – between the average import propensities for consumers' expenditure, fixed investment and exports. Those calculated for stockbuilding are not shown since the composition of stockbuilding can vary so greatly from year to year. The average import propensity for public authorities' consumption appears to be significantly lower than the others. The marginal propensities implied by the changes in the average propensities between 1954 and 1963 are shown in the final column of table 2, but little weight can be attached to them since they represent the average of changes over a nine-year period

[1] W. A. H. Godley and J. R. Shepherd, 'Forecasting imports', *National Institute Economic Review*, No. 33, August 1965.

[2] I. G. Black, J. E. Kidgell and G. F. Ray, 'Forecasting imports: a re-examination', *National Institute Economic Review*, No. 42, November 1967.

rather than the quarter-to-quarter changes in which we are principally interested.

The first relationship to investigate is thus that between the various expenditure aggregates and imports, using a time-trend to represent the influence of other factors (including relative prices). Since the net sum of expenditures gives the expenditure rather than the compromise measure of GDP (see appendix 1), the difference between the compromise and expenditure measures, assumed to represent unidentified expenditure, can also be included. Godley and Shepherd estimating over the period 1955–64 found:[1]

$$(4.7)\quad M = -358 + \underset{(0.08)}{0.30C} + \underset{(0.16)}{0.07P} + \underset{(0.08)}{0.01I} + \underset{(0.15)}{0.24X} + \underset{(0.07)}{0.52S} + \underset{(0.12)}{0.28D} + \underset{(2.3)}{1.0t}$$

$$SE = 15.9$$

where M = imports of goods and services,
C = consumers' expenditure,
P = public consumption,
I = fixed investment,
X = exports of goods and services,
S = stockbuilding,
D = discrepancy between expenditure and compromise measures of GDP,

all in £ millions at 1958 prices,

and $t = 0$ in 1959 IV.

Several of these coefficients are insignificant, although the analysis demonstrates that fluctuations in stockbuilding have a particularly high import content. When all final expenditures other than stockbuilding are added together to make up total final sales and used as a single explanatory variable, the result is:

$$(4.8)\quad M = 74 + \underset{(0.03)}{0.16F} + \underset{(0.06)}{0.55S} + \underset{(0.10)}{0.31D} + \underset{(1.5)}{3.5t}$$

$$SE = 16.5$$

where F = total final sales in £ millions at 1958 prices and all other variables are as defined for equation 4.7.

The fit is very little worse than in equation 4.7.

Godley and Shepherd found that when indicators of the pressure of demand were introduced, their effects were either insignificant or perverse (that is, they implied that a rise in the pressure of demand would lower the propensity to import). The indicators tried were unemployment and capacity utilisation (see below, chapter 7).

[1] 'Forecasting imports', *loc. cit.*, p. 36.

Price changes should have most effect in connection with imports o finished manufactures and semi-manufactures but, except for abnorma changes such as those associated with the import surcharge of 1964–6 anc with devaluation in 1967, the relevant price index has fluctuated ver little; thus probably the influence of changing relative prices is adequatel represented by a time-trend term.

The main drawback of equation 4.7 is that the estimated marginal im port propensity for total final sales of 0·16, although close to the averag propensity, is rather lower than that implied by the input–output dat in table 2. The positive constant term in equation 4.8 also implies, if th influences of other variables are assumed to be correct, that the margina import propensity is lower than the average. Godley and Shepherd triec imposing a higher coefficient for the marginal import content of total fina sales; they also tried to reintroduce the distinctions between different kind of expenditure by imposing coefficients based partly on the averag propensities derived from the 1954 input–output data and partly on th earlier regression results. These attempts gave:

$$(4.9)\quad M - 0{\cdot}19F = -136 + \underset{(0{\cdot}05)}{0{\cdot}51S} + \underset{(0{\cdot}09)}{0{\cdot}28D} + \underset{(0{\cdot}3)}{1{\cdot}9t}$$

$$SE = 16{\cdot}5$$

$$(4.10)\quad M - (0{\cdot}23C + 0{\cdot}07P + 0{\cdot}12I + 0{\cdot}21X) = -137 + \underset{(0{\cdot}05)}{0{\cdot}52S} + \underset{(0{\cdot}09)}{0{\cdot}29D} + \underset{(0{\cdot}2)}{1{\cdot}9t}$$

$$SE = 15{\cdot}5$$

where the variables are as defined for equations 4.7 and 4.8.

When these equations were re-examined in 1967, after the import surcharg had been in operation, and after successive revisions of the nationa accounts, it was found that, if the time-trend was omitted, a satisfactor value (0·22) was obtained directly for the marginal import content of tota final sales, and this simple equation now fitted better than the equation distinguishing different categories of final sales.[1] With further revisions t the national accounts data and using 1963 price series, this equation is now

$$(4.11)\quad M = -429 + 0{\cdot}322S + 0{\cdot}218F + 0{\cdot}455D$$

$$SE = 21{\cdot}6 \qquad DW = 1{\cdot}76$$

where again M = imports of goods and services,
S = stockbuilding,
F = total final sales
and D = discrepancy between expenditure and compromis GDP,
all in £ millions at 1963 prices.

[1] Black, Kidgell and Ray, 'Forecasting imports: a re-examination', *loc. cit.*, p. 53.

Some econometric work on import relationships has been done at a more disaggregated level. The end-use of the imported commodity was the main criterion used in selecting the most suitable explanatory variable: thus imports of food, beverages and finished manufactures other than machines were related to consumers' expenditure, imports of basic materials and semi-manufactures to manufacturing output (and the level of stocks in manufacturing industry), and imports of machinery and fuel to GDP. In addition, the relative prices of imports and home-produced substitutes proved to be significant in the relationships for semi-manufactures and machinery, while home and import prices separately were significant in the relationship for finished manufactures other than machinery. In the case of basic materials, import prices but not relative prices were significant (possibly because of statistical difficulties in constructing an index of the relevant home-produced competing products).

EXPORT PRICES

The prices of British exports are, in general terms, likely to be influenced by the levels of home costs, import costs and perhaps also by the state of world trade. In forecasting, prices are projected informally bearing these factors in mind. Some formal analysis of the behaviour of the prices of manufactured goods has been attempted, but with no very great success.

In this work, the price index of exports of manufactures was related to current and lagged values of home unit labour costs (defined as wages and salaries per unit of real GDP),[1] the import price index of industrial materials, and an index of the volume of world trade in manufactures. The Almon technique for estimating the lag structures was employed.[2] A typical estimated equation, in tabular form, was:

(4.12)

Variables	Weight in quarter							Sum of weights	SE of sum
	t	t–1	t–2	t–3	t–4	t–5	t–6		
Labour costs	–0·03	–0·005	0·03	0·07	0·10	0·10	0·07	0·34	(0·09)
Import costs	0·21	0·10	0·04	0·02	0·02	0·02	0·02	0·43	(0·03)
World trade	–0·05	–0·02	0·01	0·03	0·03	0·03	0·02	0·05	(0·04)

Constant = 3·88 (0·21) R^2 = 0·998 SE = 0·0028 (0·3%) DW = 2·39

where the dependent variable is export prices of manufactures (1963 = 100),

[1] As in the analysis of consumer prices (see below, chapter 5).

[2] S. Almon, 'The distributed lag between capital appropriations and expenditures', *Econometrica*, vol. 33, No. 1, January 1965.

labour costs = wage and salary bill in £ millions divided by GDP in £ millions at 1963 prices,

import costs = index of unit values of imports of industrial materials (1961 = 100)

and world trade = value in $ millions.

The estimation is in logarithms base *e* over the period 1958–67.

Clearly, this relationship has several unsatisfactory features. Among the most important are the disproportionately high weight given to import costs in comparison with home costs, and the perverse signs of the initial effects of increases in labour costs and world trade. At this stage, forecasting export prices remains a largely informal process.

IMPORT PRICES

As well as directly affecting the balance of payments, changes in import prices affect the price levels of domestic expenditures and, indirectly, via the purchasing power of overseas nations, British export prospects.[1] The construction of two indices of selected major commodities has been described in the *Review*.[2] The first index weights the commodities according to their importance in world trade, the second according to their importance in British imports. The former is thus relevant to the export prices of the primary producing countries, the latter to British import prices.

The forecast of primary producers' export prices is based partly on an informal assessment of the likely supply and demand positions in each commodity over the forecast period, partly on fairly large-scale consultation with experts, and partly on some simple econometric relationships. These relationships are aggregative, distinguishing between non-food agricultural commodities and non-ferrous metals; both are related simply to world industrial production:

$$(4.13)\quad P_a = -7{\cdot}45 + \underset{(0{\cdot}22)}{1{\cdot}21}Y; \qquad R^2 = 0{\cdot}71$$

$$(4.14)\quad P_m = -12{\cdot}42 + \underset{(0{\cdot}60)}{2{\cdot}86}Y; \qquad R^2 = 0{\cdot}64$$

where P_a = annual percentage change in price index for non-food agricultural products,

P_m = annual percentage change in price index for non-ferrous metals

and Y = annual percentage change in world industrial production.

[1] For the way in which import price indices are used in balance of payments forecasting, see below pp. 93–4.

[2] 'NIESR commodity price index numbers', *National Institute Economic Review*, No. 34, November 1965.

These crude relationships cannot take account of the complex nature of trade in commodities. Disturbances occur mainly on the supply side and they cannot be foreseen; if they affect major commodities such as sugar or copper, the relationships are quickly upset. Predicting commodity (and hence import) prices is one of the most hazardous elements in the forecasting framework. No sensible relationship at all has been developed for food prices.

Views on future trends in commodity prices form a basis for forecasting prices of three of the five major categories of British imports, separate account being taken of special agreements and regulations affecting these imports. The import price forecast for fuels is based on separate assessments of the prospects for liquid fuel prices and tanker freight rates, and that for finished manufactures on the extrapolation of past trends adjusted for any unusual change in unit labour costs in the main industrial countries.

The final stage is to translate the rates of increase in these categories of import prices, which are calculated using NIESR weights, to the corresponding series of import unit values compiled by the Department of Trade and Industry; movements of the two series are close but not identical.[1]

[1] This is confirmed by regression analysis; the regression of the government's unit value series on the NIESR series gives R^2 of 0·90 for food, 0·72 for basic materials and 0·97 for fuels.

CHAPTER 5

THE PERSONAL SECTOR

I: INCOMES AND PRICES

The personal sector's account comes into the analysis principally in determining the level of consumers' expenditure. In analysing the personal account, the main components are the generation of the different kinds of income, the analysis of price changes and the relationship between real income and real expenditure.

The *wage and salary bill* is by far the largest item in personal incomes, accounting for over 60 per cent of the total (and for even more of the variance of the total). Wages and salaries are the product of earnings per head and employment, both of which are, in turn, dependent on the pressure of demand. (The determinants of employment are discussed later, in chapter 7.) A means of analysing the behaviour of average earnings has been described by Gillion.[1] The principal hypotheses are (*a*) that the pressure of demand is normally an important determinant both of the level of wage rates and of the margin of 'drift' between negotiated rates and actual earnings, (*b*) that reductions in the negotiated working week (normal hours) have an influence on the rate of change of earnings, and (*c*) that, in the short-run at any rate, the rate of price inflation is a further influence.

Abstracting from the effect of the highly unstable 'wage-round' on the number of workers receiving increases in wage rates in a given quarter, econometric analysis has until recently suggested that the most important determinant of the rate of change of wage rates is the level of the pressure of demand;[2] the rate of change of the pressure of demand does not add significantly to the degree of explanation. The influence of the rate of price inflation is less certain; the rate of change of prices (or real wages) is significant when only the current level of the pressure of demand is included as an explanatory variable, but becomes insignificant when past values of the pressure of demand are introduced. The effect of changes in normal hours is also obscure; in different equations, values ranging from 0·3 to 0·8 were obtained for the effect on wage rates of a unit change in normal hours. Of all the equations tried, the best was:[3]

$$(5.1)\quad \dot{w} = -13{\cdot}74 + \underset{(0{\cdot}17)}{1{\cdot}69}\, n/N + \underset{(0{\cdot}29)}{0{\cdot}65}\dot{h} + \underset{(0{\cdot}08)}{0{\cdot}13}\,(o/c) + \underset{(0{\cdot}05)}{0{\cdot}10}\,(p_{-1}/p_{-5})$$

$$R^2 = 0{\cdot}82 \qquad DW = 2{\cdot}5$$

[1] C. Gillion, 'Wage-rates, earnings and wage-drift', *National Institute Economic Review*, No. 46, November 1968.

[2] As measured by the ratio of output to capacity (see below, chapter 7).

[3] Gillion, *loc. cit.*, section III.

where dotted variables indicate quarter-to-quarter percentage changes and w = index of weekly wage rates,
n/N = proportion of workers receiving wage increases,
h = normal hours,
p = index of retail prices,
o/c = index of capacity utilisation (see chapter 7).

Other equations produced marginally higher values of R^2, but only at the cost of including statistically insignificant variables.

The main determinants of average earnings (defined as wages and salaries per employee) are wage rates and the pressure of demand. Empirical analysis shows that wage rates influence earnings with a short lag;[1] this works against the hypothesis that wage rate negotiations tend to represent a formal consolidation of increases in earnings already achieved informally through drift. A unit increase in wage rates appears to lead to an increase of only about 0·6 in average wages and salaries; this is probably due partly to the fact that salary earners are not affected (or only very indirectly), and partly to the fact that minimum rates may be raised without affecting all kinds of earnings – bonus or piece-work rates, for example. The pressure of demand is a significant element in the explanation; the results suggest that an increase of 1 per cent in the pressure of demand leads to an increase of about ¼ per cent in average earnings. The constant term in these equations, representing the longer-term rate of increase in earnings independent of short-term changes in rates or in the pressure of demand, is about 2½ per cent a year. Neither the level of unemployment nor the rate of price inflation appears to affect the rate of wage-drift. The best equation was:

$$(5.2)\quad \dot{ws} = \text{constant} + \underset{(0{\cdot}12)}{0{\cdot}34\dot{w}} + \underset{(0{\cdot}12)}{0{\cdot}32\dot{w}_{-1}} + \underset{(0{\cdot}10)}{0{\cdot}25\,(o/c)}$$

$$R^2 = 0{\cdot}38$$

where $\dot{ws}$ = quarterly percentage change in wages and salaries per employee and other variables are as defined for equation 5.1.
The degree of explanation provided is clearly not very high.[2]

This empirical work was carried out using data up to the end of 1965. Since then, the kind of relationship between the pressure of demand, wage rates and wage-drift which previously existed seems to have disappeared, possibly because of the operation of various forms of a prices and incomes policy. As will be shown later (chapter 7), the relationship between the pressure of demand and employment has also been subject to substantial

[1] *Ibid.*, section IV.

[2] One factor which appears to be ignored in Gillion's empirical work is the (probably quite important) effect on the relationship between average earnings and weekly wage rates of changes in normal hours of work.

distortion since 1966. We have come to treat the movement of wage rates as exogenous, and to base the forecast on the scale of settlements made and a judgement about the influence of policy. Wage-drift has in general been greater and, at the same time, employment rather lower than might have been expected. Purely as a forecasting device therefore, we have been encouraged to put aside the breakdown of changes in the wage and salary bill into changes in rates, in drift and in employment, and to consider the movement of the wage and salary bill as a simple aggregate. The pressure of demand is the principal determinant of both employment and earnings, and it could be expected to be the main determinant of the wage and salary bill. A relationship which has been found to be tolerably satisfactory is:

$$(5.3) \quad \log_e WS = -0.145 + 0.356 \log_e \text{GDP} + 0.646 \log_e WS_{-1} + 0.00278t$$

$$R^2 = 0.999 \qquad SE = 0.0063\ (0.5\%) \qquad DW = 1.70$$

with the standard notation (see p. viii) in £ millions and $t = 0$ in 1966 1.

This equation implies that, in the context of short-term cyclical variations in the pressure of demand, an increase of 1 per cent in the rate of growth of real GDP will raise the rate of growth of the wage and salary bill, after a lag, also by about 1 per cent. The equation must, however, be regarded as far from satisfactory in general in that, apart from cyclical fluctuations, the rate of wage and salary inflation is given simply by a time-trend. It is arguable whether this accurately represents current theoretical orthodoxy.

The forecast of *current grants* from public authorities to persons is derived, in the same way as other kinds of public sector outlay, from information published by the government.

The rest of total personal income comprises mainly incomes from self-employment, incomes from dividends, incomes representing net receipts of interest, and incomes from rent. In principle, the determinants of these types of income are complex. Payments of dividends to persons, for example, will depend on the level of company profits and on companies' decisions as to the proportion of profits to be paid out as dividends. Financial factors are also likely to influence self-employment incomes and, of course, the rate of interest will be an important influence on net receipts of interest by persons. In practice, however, it is unnecessary to specify complex functions to explain the movements of these different kinds of income with a reasonably high degree of success. Most of the relevant determinants move in sympathy with the pressure of demand (with or without a lag); it has already been noted (in the chapter on investment) that profits, for example, are highly correlated with the pressure of demand. Empirically, we distinguish in the simple model only two kinds of other personal income: the first, *income from rent and from self-employment*, including the more stable elements, and the second, *income from dividends and net interest receipts*, the more volatile. In both cases, income is related to GDP. The equations are:

$$(5{\cdot}4)\quad \log_e IRSE = 0{\cdot}6464 + 0{\cdot}1566 \log_e \mathrm{GDP}_{-2} + 0{\cdot}00274t + 0{\cdot}7107 \log_e IRSE_{-1}$$

$$(5{\cdot}5)\quad \log_e DNI = -14{\cdot}61 + 2{\cdot}224 \log_e \mathrm{GDP}_{-1} + 0{\cdot}155 \log_e DNI_{-1}$$

with the standard notation (see p. viii) in £ millions and $t = 0$ in 1966 I.

The theoretical background to these equations is clearly negligible; they serve merely as convenient guide-lines pending further research. It will be seen that equation 5.4 has a much lower response to a change in GDP and that the lag is very much longer (the coefficient of lagged income being much higher) than in equation 5.5. The response to a sustained increase of 1 per cent in real GDP illustrates these differences, which are compared in table 3 with the effect on wages and salaries (equation 5.3). In addition to these responses to a change in GDP, both kinds of income grow steadily over time. If real GDP grows at about its long-term rate of 3 per cent a year, income from rent and self-employment grows at about 5·5 per cent a year, and dividends and net interest at 8·1 per cent a year. If the annual rate of growth of GDP were to slow to 2 per cent, the former would grow (in equilibrium) at 5·0 per cent, but the latter would slow to 5·3 per cent. (However, these differential growth rates are illustrative only; there is no suggestion that they could be sustained indefinitely.)

Table 3. *Effects on types of personal income at current prices of a 1 per cent quarterly increase in real GDP*

Percentages

Quarter	Wages and salaries	Income from rent and self-employment	Dividends and net interest
1	0·36	—	—
2	0·59	—	2·24
3	0·73	0·16	2·59
4	0·83	0·26	2·64
5	0·89	0·35	2·65
∞	1·00	0·54	2·65

The final elements of total personal income are employers' contributions both to the National Insurance and associated funds and to private pension schemes, and forces' pay. Employers' National Insurance contributions are subsequently deducted, since they are not disposable income, and thus net out of the account entirely. Employers' contributions to private schemes remain in the total of personal incomes as an imputed element. Employees' National Insurance and Health contributions are of course deducted from total incomes in calculating personal disposable income. It follows that it is possible for simplicity to forecast only the balance of these contributions – that is, employers' private contributions *less* employees' National Insurance contributions. Of these, the first is a very trend-like series while the second changes sharply when contribution rates are changed. The balance, *net insurance contributions*, thus shows an underlying trend modified by occasional sharp changes. This balance is treated as an exogenous element. *Forces' pay* is similarly treated as an exogenous component since changes depend almost exclusively on government reviews of rates of pay.

The main deduction from personal income made before it is allocated between consumption and saving is direct taxation. As well as income tax collected through the pay as you earn (PAYE) scheme, this includes income tax and surtax paid by the recipients of income themselves, as well as taxes on dividends and interest paid at source by companies and by public corporations and authorities.

The two main factors of which account has to be taken in analysing the relationship of taxes to income are the distinction made between types of income (specifically, between earned and unearned income) and the progressiveness of the tax rates. The first means that, on a given individual's income, the marginal tax rate will be higher if the income is unearned than if it is earned, while the second means that, over time, there is a secular rise in both marginal tax rates as aggregate incomes rise even if statutory tax rates remain constant. Although a complete model of the direct tax system would have to be highly complex to take account of all the factors involved, a satisfactory degree of explanation of aggregate tax payments can be achieved very simply.

First, distinctions are drawn between wage and salary incomes, current grant incomes, and all other incomes. This corresponds in part to a distinction between earned incomes (wages and salaries) and unearned incomes (all others), and in part to a crude breakdown by level of income, since, per head, average other incomes are higher than average wage and salary incomes, which, in turn, are higher than average incomes from current grants.

The corresponding breakdown of taxes by type of income on which they are levied is only available annually. Certain simplifying assumptions are necessary in order to construct a quarterly series. First, current grant incomes are assumed to give rise to no tax liability. This is a valid assumption in almost every case where an individual's income consists entirely of current grants, but it is not valid where current grants (notably family allowances) are received in addition to other kinds of income. Secondly, all income tax collected under the PAYE scheme is regarded as levied on wages and salaries; in addition, a proportion of surtax is also allocated to wages and salaries.[1] Finally, all other personal tax payments are assumed to be levied on other personal incomes.

The average tax rate on wages and salaries has shown a fairly strong upward trend, and there have been frequent sharp changes associated with changes in tax rates and allowances in successive budgets. The average rate on other personal income has risen much more slowly, though at a higher level. Because of the frequent changes in the tax structure, the task of estimating the tax functions econometrically is extremely difficult. In forecasting, where tax rates are specifically assumed to remain unchanged,[2] it is possible simply to use rough 'rules of thumb', taking the average tax rates at the latest date as given and assuming that the underlying trend rate of increase in the marginal tax rate (reflecting the effect of the progressive structure of the tax system as aggregate incomes rise) will continue. These rules of thumb are:

$$(5.6)\quad TAXWS = -583 + (0{\cdot}24 + 0{\cdot}001t)WS$$

$$(5.7)\quad TAXO = -301 + 0{\cdot}33IRSE + 0{\cdot}40DNI$$

with the standard notation (see p. viii) in £ millions,

where $TAX = TAXWS + TAXO$

and $t = 0$ in 1966 I.

A final small leakage from total personal income is net transfers by persons abroad – migrants' remittances, gifts, and so on. This small quantity is forecast as part of the balance of payments analysis (see below, chapter 9).

RETAIL AND CONSUMER PRICES

The consumer price index, used to deflate the value of consumers' expenditure to volume terms in the national accounts, is a current-weighted index. This means that the deflator is sensitive not only to changes in individual prices, but also to changes in the pattern of expenditure. From the point of view of the analysis of price movements, it is clearly easier to abstract from these changes due to shifts in expenditure patterns and to concentrate on a base-weighted price index. The retail price index of the Department

[1] For the years up to 1962 this proportion is shown annually in the Blue Book (Central Statistical Office, *National Income and Expenditure*, HMSO, annual) but from 1963 it is estimated.

[2] The method of treating *changes* in the tax rates is dealt with below, in chapter 8.

of Employment (formerly the Ministry of Labour) comes a little closer to this requirement: it is chain-weighted – that is, the weights used are constant for each year and are revised each January on the basis of expenditure patterns over the previous three years as revealed by the annual Family Expenditure Survey. The Survey is based on a sample of families whose income is below a certain level (currently £40 a week); the coverage of the index is thus less than exhaustive and, in particular, the exclusion of high-income families probably means that services, the prices of which increase relatively fast, are underweighted when the index is regarded as an economy-wide indicator of the price level.[1]

The retail price index is available in some detail for different kinds of expenditure. For purposes of analysis, it is important to distinguish between prices which are determined by special influences, notably those of food and housing, and prices which are determined by the levels of costs and of demand in the economy generally. The latter make up only a little over half of the index for all items. The following analysis is a summary of the work described in detail by Godley and Rowe.[2]

Some food prices are subject to strong seasonal influences, especially fruit, vegetables, eggs and some kinds of meat. These seasonal factors vary from year to year according to whether supplies of the items are good or bad, and are inherently difficult to analyse and virtually impossible to forecast. Apart from these fluctuations, the trend of these food prices has been broadly in line with the trend of other prices, and in forecasting this trend is projected.

Housing prices – rent, rates and repair costs – also have a strong seasonal element, principally because local authority rates are changed annually between March and June. Apart from these seasonal movements, there has been a steady upward trend in housing prices; the analysis of this trend has not been attempted and simple extrapolation has tended to produce reasonably successful forecasts.

The remainder of the retail price index covers non-seasonal food prices (making up just over 20 per cent of the index) and all other prices (just over 60 per cent). The hypothesis used in analysing the movements of these prices is essentially that evolved by Neild:[3] entrepreneurs set prices by assessing their costs on the basis of 'normal' or 'full' capacity operation and adding a profit margin determined by convention. This theory implies that prices are not influenced by short-run cyclical changes in the pressure of demand or by short-run cyclical variations in productivity. The first of these would tend to raise prices in times of rapid expansion, while the

[1] For a full account of the retail price index, see Ministry of Labour, *Method of construction and calculation of the index of retail prices*, 4th ed., HMSO, 1967.

[2] W. A. H. Godley and D. A. Rowe, 'Retail and consumer prices, 1955–1963', *National Institute Economic Review*, No. 30, November 1964.

[3] R. R. Neild, *Pricing and Employment in the Trade Cycle*, Cambridge University Press, 1963.

second would operate in the opposite direction; the possibility that prices are sensitive in both ways but to a self-cancelling degree is not ruled out. A cyclical element in prices is retained, however, because wage rates tend to rise faster the higher the pressure of demand, even though the 'normal cost' hypothesis means that cyclical changes in wage-earnings attributable to changes in the extent of overtime working are excluded. Prices also respond directly to some changes in indirect tax rates – purchase tax, tobacco and alcohol duties, and so on – and indirectly to other changes in indirect tax rates in so far as these affect business costs in a way which is passed on to consumers in the form of higher prices. An increase in motor fuel duties or in motor licence rates, for example, will affect transport costs, and some of this increase is likely to be reflected ultimately in higher prices to final buyers including consumers. Finally, increases in the costs of imports will affect retail prices. Again, this influence may be direct, where consumers purchase goods produced abroad, or indirect, where imported materials enter into domestic production of consumer goods.

In the analysis of price behaviour, it is first necessary to remove from the price series the effects of changes in tax rates, since these changes are regarded as determined wholly exogenously. In the case of direct effects, the change can be assessed reasonably precisely simply by examining the behaviour of the relevant elements of the retail price index at the time of the change. For indirect effects an assumption has to be made. Generally, it is assumed that about half of the increase in revenue paid directly by business will ultimately be passed on to consumers as higher prices, and that this will happen only gradually, taking nine months or a year to be fully passed on.[1]

In the original analysis,[2] information supplied in confidence by the Ministry of Labour made it possible to use a retail price series excluding prices of second-hand cars and nationalised industries' output, which are not cost-determined, as well as food and housing prices. Two import price series were used. The first covered basic materials and fuels (weighted according to the pattern of consumers' expenditure) and the second (similarly weighted) covered imports of manufactures, whose prices might be expected to have a very rapid effect on the retail price index.

Following the 'normal cost' hypothesis, the index of labour costs ought to be average weekly wages and salaries of workers in the relevant industries, corrected for cyclical variation in the level of overtime working and divided by the longer-term trend in productivity. But the lack of adequate data prohibited the construction of such an index without substantial approximations. First, earnings in the relevant industries were assumed to

[1] See W. A. B. Hopkin and W. A. H. Godley, 'An analysis of tax changes', *National Institute Economic Review*, No. 32, May 1965, p. 36.

[2] Godley and Rowe, *loc. cit.*

move exactly as earnings in all industries – almost certainly a justifiable assumption. Secondly, in the absence of changes in normal hours, overtime-corrected earnings were assumed to be systematically related to wage rates; specifically, changes in these earnings were assumed to be proportionate to changes in wage rates together with a trend to allow earnings to rise faster than rates. Decreases in normal hours were also included: it was assumed that part of any reduction would affect only the balance between standard and overtime hours (thus increasing labour costs more than an equal percentage rise in wage rates) and that any associated change in productivity would not be enough to offset this. The best assumption for purposes of estimation turned out to be that a cut in normal hours raises labour costs by 1·3 times as much as an equal percentage rise in wage rates.

The form of regression equation estimated for this section of the retail price index was thus:

$$(5.8) \quad p = a + b_1 m_1 + b_2 m_2 + b_3 w / [h^a (1 + r)^t] + b_4 p_{-1}$$

and the best result obtained by regression analysis was:

$$(5.9) \quad p = 13{\cdot}743 + \underset{(0{\cdot}003)}{0{\cdot}189} \, [w / (h^{1\cdot3} . \, 1{\cdot}0097^t . \, 1{\cdot}0003^{t^2})]_{-1}$$

$$+ \underset{(0{\cdot}009)}{0{\cdot}050} (m_1)_{-2} + \underset{(0{\cdot}024)}{0{\cdot}081} (m_2)_{-1} - \underset{(0{\cdot}025)}{0{\cdot}060} (m_2)_{-2} + \underset{(0{\cdot}069)}{0{\cdot}609} p_{-1}$$

$R^2 = 0{\cdot}99 \qquad SE = 0{\cdot}177 \qquad DW = 2{\cdot}27$

where p = index of retail prices other than food, housing, nationalised industries' output and second-hand cars,
m_1 = index of import prices of fuels and basic materials,
m_2 = index of import prices of manufactures,
w = index of weekly wage rates
and h = index of normal working hours.

The accelerating trend in the wage-cost variable was added to reflect the apparent acceleration in the rate of growth of productivity in the economy as a whole.

The cost structure implied by these coefficients seems acceptable. The weights given to wage and import costs are in the ratio of about 5 to 2, corresponding well with estimates based directly on input–output data. Changes in wage costs affect prices with a fairly extended lag, with about three-quarters of the full effect of a change taking place in a year. Changes in the prices of imported manufactured goods have the fullest impact in the subsequent quarter, while changes in the prices of basic materials and fuels have a similar lag to that of wage costs, but slightly longer delayed. The trend term reflecting both productivity and wage-drift was not directly estimated by the regression analysis, and different figures would give only marginally worse explanations of price movements.

The high degree of explanation given by this relationship provides evidence that the pressure of demand has no readily apparent influence (or mutually cancelling influences) on the level of prices, except in so far as it affects the rate of growth of wage rates or, more problematically, of longer-term productivity. Apart from these possibilities, assertions that a high pressure of demand directly causes inflation (or conversely lowers prices by lowering unit costs) are shown to be unnecessary hypotheses, at any rate in the short term, in explaining price movements.

The relationship between the retail price index and the implicit deflator of consumers' expenditure in the national accounts (the consumer price index) is determined partly by questions of coverage and partly by their different weighting. To the extent that the retail price index underestimates fast-rising service prices, the consumer price index will rise the faster: on the other hand, the slow response of the weights used in the retail price index to changes in the pattern of expenditure means that, in so far as changes in relative prices cause changes in the pattern of consumption, the retail price index will rise the faster. Godley and Rowe related the two indices for three categories of consumers' expenditure.[1] The regression estimates they obtained were:

(5.10) *Food:*

$$C_f = \underset{(0.053)}{0.660}\, P_f + \underset{(0.0003)}{0.0010}\, t + \text{seasonals}$$

$$R^2 = 0.983$$

Housing:

$$C_h = \underset{(0.045)}{0.965}\, P_h + \underset{(0.0006)}{0.0006}\, t + \text{seasonals}$$

$$R^2 = 0.9995$$

Other prices:

$$C_o = \underset{(0.041)}{0.862}\, P_o - \underset{(0.0003)}{0.0011}\, t + \text{seasonals}$$

$$R^2 = 0.995$$

where C = consumer price index
and P = retail price index,
both as index numbers with 1958 = 100.

Using these relationships, a forecast of the total consumer price index can be derived, via retail prices, from the projections of wage rates, hours and import prices.

In recent years, broadly speaking from 1965–6 onwards, this system of

[1] 'Retail and consumer prices, 1955–1963', *loc. cit.*

pricing equations has persistently overestimated the rate of increase of prices. An alternative, much simpler system has therefore been tried. The most direct measure of actual (as opposed to trend) unit labour costs is clearly wages and salaries per unit of output – in national income accounting terms, the wage and salary bill divided by GDP at constant prices. Using this and import prices in a price equation (with the consumer price index net of the estimated effects of indirect tax changes) gives:

$$(5.11) \quad CPIFC = \underset{(0.094)}{0.318\,WS/\mathrm{GDP}} + \underset{(0.021)}{0.046\,MP} + \underset{(0.076)}{0.762\,CPIFC_{-1}}$$

$$R^2 = 0.999 \qquad SE = 0.48\% \qquad DW = 2.71$$

with the standard notation (see p. viii).

Despite the extreme simplicity of this relationship, the standard error is reasonably low and appears to be less than double that associated with the highly complex set of relationships described earlier.

The coefficients of lagged prices in equation 5.11 imply a rather rapid adjustment of the price level to an increase in unit wage and salary costs, with about a quarter of the final induced price increase occurring during the same quarter as the cost increase, nearly half by the end of the second quarter, and two-thirds by the end of the year. A more sophisticated technique of analysing the lag structure, due to Almon, has been tried.[1] The results tend to confirm, if not strengthen, the view that price increases follow cost increases more rapidly than has often been supposed.[2]

[1] 'The distributed lag between capital appropriations and expenditures', *loc. cit.*

[2] *National Institute Economic Review*, No. 52, May 1970, pp. 17–18.

CHAPTER 6

THE PERSONAL SECTOR

II: CONSUMPTION

Consumers' expenditure (consumption, for short) is determined partly by consumers' incomes and partly by the extent to which consumers are willing (or able) to increase their net burden of indebtedness.

CREDIT

In a really full model of consumers' behaviour, it would be reasonable to look for a formal analysis of the factors influencing the relationship between the levels of debt and of income. In practice, it is hard to give such a formal account. There are two main sources of credit open to consumers – hire purchase debt and personal bank credit. Hire purchase contracts are subject to two powerful instruments of government control: regulation of the minimum percentage deposit to be paid and the maximum period of repayment. Changes in these regulations will affect the demand for credit strongly by changing the amount of money to be saved for the deposit before a product can be acquired and by changing the monthly repayment for a given volume of debt. In practice, changes in these regulations in Britain have been so frequent that their effects have dominated past movements in the level of net debt, and it is virtually impossible to identify the influence of other factors. It seems likely that, as incomes rise, consumers will wish to devote a constant (or perhaps a rising) proportion of their incomes to servicing debt. This implies that, in the aggregate and in the absence of changes in regulations, the volume of debt would rise steadily in line with, or a little faster than, the rate of increase of incomes. But to estimate such a trend, abstracting from the effects of the frequent sharp changes due to government action (and possibly the effects of 'echoes' of earlier changes as contracts expire), has not proved possible.

Personal bank credit has, in practice, tended to move broadly in line with hire purchase credit, even though government control (at any rate from the demand side) is rather weaker. It seems likely that these sympathetic movements result largely from informal guidance given by the government to the banks on desirable increases in lending, particularly to the personal sector. In the last few years, government attempts to impose ceilings on lending by both banks and finance houses have had some effect in restraining rates of increase. Again, formal analysis of this aspect has proved very difficult and only rough estimates of the likely effects have been made.

Movements in personal credit, then, are perforce treated as exogenously induced in both analysis and forecasting. In tracing the effect of these movements they are treated as if they were a form of income (see below).

INCOME AND EXPENDITURE

In the previous chapter, the analysis of various kinds of income and of the personal tax liabilities to which they give rise was described, as was the analysis of consumer prices. In what follows, it is assumed that all variables have been deflated by the consumer price index and are thus expressed in real terms.

In the analysis of the relation between aggregate incomes and consumption,[1] incomes are broken down three ways into wages and salaries, current grants and other personal incomes. On the whole, recipients of current grants save less, and recipients of other personal incomes more, than wage and salary earners.[2] We should expect, that is, differing marginal propensities to consume to be associated with the different kinds of income.

We would also expect some lag in the adjustment of the level of consumption to a change in the level of income. Such lags could arise in several ways – as a simple adjustment taking some time, as the result of reluctance to depart from a 'habitual' level of consumption, or as the result of a 'permanent income' hypothesis in which permanent income depends only partially on actual current income. A simple version of each of these hypotheses is to postulate that the current quarter's consumption depends partly on the current quarter's income and partly on the previous quarter's consumption.[3] It is possible that the length of this lag will also differ between kinds of income, with the (relatively) poor responding more immediately to a change in income than the (relatively) rich. Finally, there is unlikely to be any lag between a change in debt, as measured here, and the associated change in consumption, since credit facilities are normally negotiated to finance specific purchases.

The best relationship found between all these factors was:

$$(6.1)\quad C' = 130 + \underset{(0{\cdot}136)}{0{\cdot}456C'_{-1}} + \underset{(0{\cdot}133)}{0{\cdot}762Yw'} - \underset{(0{\cdot}160)}{0{\cdot}269Yw'_{-1}} + \underset{(0{\cdot}162)}{0{\cdot}403Yo} - \underset{(1{\cdot}35)}{1{\cdot}94\,t}$$

$$R^2 = 0{\cdot}999 \qquad SE = 25{\cdot}9\ (0{\cdot}65\%) \qquad DW = 2{\cdot}10$$

[1] For a fuller account, see M. J. C. Surrey, 'Personal incomes and consumers' expenditure', in Hilton and Heathfield (eds.), *The Econometric Study of the United Kingdom*.

[2] Principally because the average income of current grant recipients is likely to be lower, and that of the recipients of other (self-employed or unearned) incomes higher, than the wage or salary earner's. But other socio-economic factors such as family size may also be reflected.

[3] See Surrey, *loc. cit.*, for a demonstration that the different hypotheses referred to yield the same form for purposes of estimation.

where Yw′ = wage and salary bill *plus* forces' pay *less* employees' National Insurance contributions *less* tax payments *plus* 1·1 times current grants,

Yo = all other personal income *plus* employers' private contributions *less* net transfers abroad, *less* other National Insurance contributions *less* tax payments,

C′ = consumers' expenditure *less* 0·9 times Δ credit (change in credit), where credit is a weighted sum equal to 100 per cent of hire purchase credit and 50 per cent of personal and professional bank advances,[1]

all quarterly and seasonally adjusted, in £ millions deflated by the consumer price index (1958 = 100) to 1958 prices,

and t = time-trend 1 per quarter from 1955 to 1961, constant thereafter.

In the empirical work it proved impossible to separate the lag structures for current grants and for wage and salary incomes, so they were formed into the combined variable defined for equation 6.1.[2] This relationship can best be summarised by the effects which it implies for consumption when the different kinds of income increase by £100 million in a quarter and then grow as before. These effects are shown in table 4.

Table 4. *Effects on consumption of £100 million increases in disposable incomes and credit*

£ millions

Quarter	Wages and salaries	Current grants	Other personal incomes	Credit
1	76	84	40	90
2	84	92	59	—
3	88	97	67	—
4	89	98	71	—
5	90	99	73	—
6+	90	99	74	—

SOURCE: NIESR estimates.

Given that the average propensity to consume is about 92 per cent, these figures confirm the hypothesis that different marginal propensities can

[1] These weights and the coefficient of 0·9 applied to the composite variable were based partly on other empirical work and partly on *a priori* reasoning (see Surrey, *loc. cit.*).

[2] Surrey, *loc. cit.*

plausibly be ascribed to the different kinds of income, with the overall marginal propensity being close to the average propensity.

The coefficient standard errors shown in equation 6.1 indicate, however, that these marginal propensities are only just significantly different. When the equation was re-estimated on later (and revised) data, startlingly different results were obtained:

$$(6.2)\quad C' = 188 + \underset{(0{\cdot}157)}{0{\cdot}112C'_{-1}} + \underset{(0{\cdot}116)}{0{\cdot}873Yw'} + \underset{(0{\cdot}192)}{0{\cdot}069Yw'_{-1}} + \underset{(0{\cdot}194)}{0{\cdot}098Yo} - \underset{(2{\cdot}66)}{3{\cdot}47t}$$

$$R^2 = 0{\cdot}999 \qquad SE = 32{\cdot}1\ (0{\cdot}65\%) \qquad DW = 2{\cdot}24$$

with variables as defined for equation 6.1, but deflated to 1963, not 1958 prices.

In 6.2, not only are the values of the coefficients different from those in 6.1, they are, except for that of Yw′, all insignificant statistically. Because of the strong *a priori* reasons for believing in the importance of distinguishing between the different kinds of income, further investigations were made with restricting assumptions and provided the following relationship, in which the coefficient of 0·4 for Yo was imposed:

$$(6.3)\quad C' = 259 + \underset{(0{\cdot}098)}{0{\cdot}449C'_{-1}} + \underset{(0{\cdot}104)}{0{\cdot}472Yw'} + 0{\cdot}4Yo$$

$$R^2 = 0{\cdot}999 \qquad SE = 29{\cdot}2\ (0{\cdot}57\%) \qquad DW = 1{\cdot}98$$

with variables as defined for equation 6.2.

Equation 6.3 gives an equilibrium marginal propensity to consume out of disposable wages and salaries of 0·86 and out of other disposable income of 0·73, both within the limits of *a priori* acceptability.

This experience of the instability of estimated consumption functions with respect to changes in the data due to revisions of the official statistics serves as a salutary reminder of the difficulties inherent in the construction of macro-economic models to fit reality. Of course, the relationship in question – in the present case the consumption function – may have been specified incorrectly. In particular, important explanatory variables may have been omitted. But this does not eliminate the problem; there are strong *a priori* reasons for believing that the kind of consumption function described above should be reasonably robust, and it seems odd that any omitted factor should be either of overriding importance or particularly sensitive to revisions of the data. No convincing solution has yet been found and the experience remains a reminder of the tentative nature of the model of the economy which is being described.

THE FACTOR COST ADJUSTMENT

The factor cost adjustment represents the net indirect tax content of expenditure at 1963 prices.[1] The use of 1963 prices implies the assumption of tax rates ruling in 1963.[2] In practice, much the greatest part of the total of indirect taxes on expenditure is levied on consumers' expenditure (just over 83 per cent in the base year 1963) and it is a reasonable assumption in a simple model to relate the factor cost adjustment to consumption only. A very simple relationship established by regression analysis is:

$$(6.4)\qquad \Delta FCA = -2 + \underset{(0{\cdot}031)}{0{\cdot}309}\Delta CE$$

$$R^2 = 0{\cdot}70 \qquad SE = 12{\cdot}8 \qquad DW = 2{\cdot}13$$

with the standard notation (see p. viii) in £ millions.

This implies a rather high marginal tax content of consumption,[3] slightly offset by the downward trend in the factor cost adjustment represented by the small negative constant term.

[1] That is indirect taxes less subsidies, the latter being conveniently thought of in the present context as negative indirect taxes.

[2] The factor cost adjustment is thus the indirect tax content of expenditure at constant (1963) tax rates.

[3] 31 per cent, which may reflect the omission of other kinds of expenditure from the equation.

CHAPTER 7

EMPLOYMENT, UNEMPLOYMENT AND PRODUCTIVE POTENTIAL

One of the central aims of short-term economic forecasting is to predict the movement of total output in relation to the supply capacity of the economy. The foregoing chapters have been concerned with demands made on output and on imports; the measurement of changes in supply capacity has so far scarcely been considered.

In the simplest theoretical terms, with labour and capital as homogeneous and substitutable factors of production, economists write the relationship between output and factor inputs as a production function whose most general expression simply states that output can be considered as some function of labour and capital. This relationship can be taken to apply either to the actual situation obtaining, relating the employed factors to produced output or, more relevantly in the present context, as a capacity relation showing, for the total capital stock in existence and the total available supply of labour, the output which *could* be produced if both were fully employed. Technical progress, the ability of the economy to produce more over time even with fixed factor inputs, can be most simply incorporated by including a time-trend in the relationship. In practical terms, there are daunting problems in trying to estimate any of these forms interpreted in the sense of supply capacity. First, the available data on capital stock are severely limited; secondly, the full-employment, as distinct from recorded, values of the other variables do not exist. Substantial progress can be made, however, if we adopt the familiar definition of the short period as that in which the influence of changes in the stock of capital can be ignored. In this case, a simpler relationship between labour supply and output is assumed. On the labour side, use can be made of actual employment and unemployment statistics in deriving a measure of the factor input.

This is the approach adopted in short-term forecasting and described in detail by Godley and Shepherd.[1] Growth of supply capacity (or of productive potential) is defined as that level of output which would maintain a constant level of unemployment, regardless of whether there are any associated changes in capital utilisation. In the empirical analysis there are two main relationships: between output and employment, and between employment and unemployment.

The relationship between employment and unemployment, as well as

[1] W. A. H. Godley and J. R. Shepherd, 'Long-term growth and short-term policy', *National Institute Economic Review*, No. 29, August 1964.

depending on the demographic changes in the number of people of working age, also depends on participation rates and on the relationship between the actual change in unemployment and the number of people who *register* as unemployed. The statistics of employment and unemployment since 1955 reveal two characteristics: first, the short-term fluctuations in employment are much greater than those in unemployment; secondly, until 1966 employment grew substantially, while unemployment did not.

The first phenomenon – larger fluctuations in employment than in unemployment – is explained by the unregistered unemployed. These are various groups of marginal workers, particularly married women and retired people, who enter employment only in periods of high demand for labour, but who do not register as unemployed if dismissed as the pressure of demand falls. This unregistered unemployment can be presumed to move closely with registered unemployment.

The upward trend in employment is explained by the net effect of increases in the numbers of people in those age and sex groups which make up the working population (that is, by demographic changes), and by those changes in participation rates which are not associated with changes in the pressure of demand but depend largely on social factors, such as the duration of full-time education, the average size of families and the age at which women have their children. These factors can reasonably be assumed to change fairly smoothly and continuously over time and to be adequately represented by a time-trend, although special allowances may need to be made for identifiable sudden changes (for example, the projected raising of the school-leaving age from 15 to 16 years).

Empirical analysis of the relationship between employment and unemployment thus relates employment net of the demographic contribution (measured at constant participation rates) to unemployment and to various forms of time-trend representing changes in participation rates. Shepherd[1] found that a good explanation was obtained using:

$$(7.1) \quad E - D = 30{,}866 - 1{,}639 \log_{10} U + \underset{(1{\cdot}9)}{30{\cdot}93t} - \underset{(3{\cdot}8)}{30{\cdot}38t'}$$

$$SE = 57 \qquad DW = 0{\cdot}43$$

where E = employment in thousands,
D = demographic contribution at mid-1951 participation rates,
U = unemployment in thousands,
t = time-trend rising 1 per quarter, with 1955 I = 1,
and t' = time-trend 0 to 1960 IV, then rising 1 per quarter.

The log-linear relationship between unemployment and employment was found to give a better fit than a linear one; it implies that a change in

[1] J. R. Shepherd, 'Productive potential and the demand for labour', *Economic Trends*, No. 178, August 1968.

employment of 100,000 (about 0·4 per cent) is associated with a change in registered unemployment of only 36,000 when unemployment is about 1 per cent, but of 88,000 when unemployment is as high as $2\frac{1}{2}$ per cent. This reflects the fact that, at times of very full employment, it is the marginal groups of workers least likely to register who are most affected by hiring and firing, but as unemployment rises most of those affected are intra-marginal workers whose dependence on their income is likely to make them register as unemployed.

Equation 7.1 can be rearranged to provide an estimate of the levels of employment required over time if unemployment is to remain constant at some (arbitrary) fixed level. This calculated level of employment may be termed the supply of labour, supply being interpreted in the sense of constant capacity utilisation in which it is required for capacity estimates. Taking the arbitrary fixed rate of unemployment as $1\frac{1}{4}$ per cent of the labour supply, we obtain:

$$(7.2) \quad L - D = 30{,}866 - 1{,}639 \log_{10}(0{\cdot}125L) + 30{\cdot}93t - 30{\cdot}38t'$$

or

$$(7.3) \quad L + 1{,}639 \log_{10}(0{\cdot}125L) = 30{,}866 + 30{\cdot}93t - 30{\cdot}38t' + D$$

where L = labour supply in thousands
and other variables are as defined for equation 7.1.
This may be solved by an iterative method.

EMPLOYMENT AND OUTPUT

The way in which employment responds to a change in output can be considered in two stages. First, there is a new equilibrium level of employment corresponding to the new level of output. This equilibrium level will depend on the level of output, on changes in productivity both over time and in relation to the pressure of demand, and on changes in normal working hours. Secondly, actual employment will adjust only gradually to equilibrium employment since hiring and firing take some time.

Fluctuations in employment have been smaller than fluctuations in output. This suggests that there is an apparent gain in productivity as the pressure of demand rises, attributable partly to the fact that some employees are regarded as an overhead – a short-term rise in output does not increase their numbers – and partly to increases in overtime working by existing employees. Thus the percentage change in employment is lower than the percentage change in output. Apart from this cyclical productivity effect, it is assumed that underlying productivity has grown in a smooth way, represented by various time-trends, and that the remaining recorded changes in productivity are attributable solely to the lag in the adjustment of actual to equilibrium unemployment.

The relationship is also affected by changes in the labour supply and by changes in normal hours of work. Changes in the labour supply are unlikely to affect productive capacity to the full extent immediately, since new workers will take time to train and will only gradually reach their full productivity. But it turns out to be impossible to estimate statistically the rate at which this happens, and the plausible assumption is made that about half the potential productivity is attained immediately, rising to three-quarters after one year. Reductions in normal (formally negotiated) hours of work will also have a complicated effect on capacity. Such reductions affect only about 50 per cent of the labour force; they are partially offset by both increased overtime working and increased productivity. It is assumed that only a quarter of such cuts are effective in terms of reducing productive potential.

These assumptions can be summarised in the form of a relationship:

(7.4) $$E^* - L = k + a_1 (P - \tfrac{1}{2}L - \tfrac{1}{4}L_{-4} - \tfrac{1}{4}H) + a_2 t + a_3 t''$$

where E^* = 'equilibrium' employment in thousands,
L = labour supply in thousands,
P = GDP index (1958 = 100),
H = normal working hours index (1958 = 100),
t = time-trend rising 1 per quarter, with 1955 I = 1,
and t'' = time-trend 0 to 1960 II, then rising 1 per quarter.

Here the change in equilibrium employment net of the change in the labour supply depends on the change in output net of the assumed actual influence of changes in the labour supply and normal hours, and on productivity trends. The adjustment process of actual to equilibrium unemployment is found to be best represented by a discontinuous process, with a slower response to large changes than to small ones. The estimated equation and adjustment process are:

(7.5) $$\log_{10}E^* - \log_{10}L = 0{\cdot}8055 \log_{10}L + 0{\cdot}4442 (\log_{10}P - \tfrac{1}{2}\log_{10}L - \tfrac{1}{4}\log_{10}L_{-4} - \tfrac{1}{4}\log_{10}H) - 0{\cdot}00119t - 0{\cdot}00030t''$$

$$SE = 0{\cdot}00137\ (0{\cdot}3\%) \qquad DW = 1{\cdot}11$$

(7.6) $$E - E_{-1} = 0{\cdot}7(E^* - E_{-1}), \text{ for } E^* - E_{-1} \leqslant 30$$
$$E - E_{-1} = 13{\cdot}5 + 0{\cdot}25(E^* - E_{-1}), \text{ for } E^* - E_{-1} \geqslant 30$$

where E = actual employment in thousands
and other variables are as defined for equation 7.4.

Thus equations 7.5 and 7.6 can be used, together with an estimate of the labour supply and normal hours, to forecast employment from the movement of GDP. Equation 7.1, rearranged, can then be used to draw the implications for the movement of unemployment.

PRODUCTIVE POTENTIAL

By definition, the growth of productive potential (or of capacity) is given by the rate at which output could rise without altering the level of unemployment,[1] which, given the definition of labour supply used in equation 7.2, means the rate of growth of output which will allow employment to grow in line with the labour supply. Rearrangement of equation 7.5 to provide this estimate gives:

$$(7.7)\quad \log_{10}C = \tfrac{1}{2}\log_{10}L + \tfrac{1}{4}\log_{10}L_{-4} + \tfrac{1}{4}\log_{10}H - 1{\cdot}81321 + 0{\cdot}00268t + 0{\cdot}00067t''$$

where C = productive potential index (1963 adjusted to $1\tfrac{1}{4}\%$ unemployment = 100)

and the other variables are as defined for equation 7.4.

One complication is that the assumptions made about the effect of increases in the supply of labour imply that, even in the long term, a change of 1 per cent in the labour supply only changes productive potential by $\tfrac{3}{4}$ per cent. In order to correct this, the equation 7.7 can be adapted to fit the assumption that, after three years, changes in the labour supply are fully reflected in productive potential. The productivity trends have then to be adjusted to give the same growth over past periods as the estimated equation. This gives (with the notation in 7.7):

$$(7.8)\quad \log_{10}C = \tfrac{1}{2}\log_{10}L + \tfrac{1}{4}\log_{10}L_{-4} + \tfrac{1}{8}(\log_{10}L_{-8} + \log_{10}L_{-12}) - 2{\cdot}90311 + 0{\cdot}00247t + 0{\cdot}00067t''$$

The employment equation can be similarly adjusted.

Equation 7.8 implies that underlying productivity per head (productive potential net of the effect of changes in the labour supply) was growing by about 2·3 per cent per annum between 1955 and 1960 and at about 2·9 per cent in the next five years. After allowing for changes in labour supply, the overall productive potential of the economy was rising at about 2·8 per cent per annum in the earlier period, and by about 3·4 per cent in the later period. Since 1966, with the labour supply ceasing to grow, the rate of increase of productive potential is estimated to have fallen back to a little under 3 per cent per annum.

[1] There are, of course, other definitions, see p. 16n.

CHAPTER 8
THE COMPLETE MODEL

The foregoing chapters have described the ways in which each of the aggregates making up the expenditure account of the national income is related to the rest and to other factors; this system of relationships as a whole was shown diagrammatically in the flow charts.[1] The system comprises a number of exogenous elements – exports, public expenditure, and so on – together with a simultaneously determined bloc in which, for example, consumers' expenditure as an element of demand influences GDP which, in turn, through the pressure of demand, affects incomes and prices and hence is a determinant of the level of consumers' expenditure.

If this system were wholly linear, it would comprise a number of simultaneous linear equations with, in general, a unique solution which could be found quite simply by solving the set in the familiar way. In fact, the system is non-linear in a number of important instances. This is ensured, for example, by the use of price indices, where the relation between value on the one hand and volume and price on the other is multiplicative, and by the inclusion of log-linear relationships. These non-linearities make the solution far more complex. Essentially, it is necessary to solve the system for given values of the exogenous variables by a process of successive approximation. A trial solution for GDP is taken, the values of the endogenous variables based on this trial value of GDP are calculated and the resulting GDP total compared with the initial trial value. On the basis of the discrepancy so revealed, a second trial value for GDP is taken and the process is repeated until consistency is achieved.[2]

To perform the iterative procedure by hand can be extremely arduous, although until very recently there was no real alternative. But the accessibility of computer facilities makes it possible to solve the system in essentially the same fashion in a matter of seconds. The remainder of this chapter describes, first informally and then formally, the specification and solution of the model in its current form for forecasting purposes.

SPECIFICATION OF THE MODEL

The somewhat blurred line between exogenously and endogenously determined elements has already been discussed. In the simplest form of the

[1] See pp. 23 and 24.

[2] An alternative approach is to linearise the system by means of approximate linear expansions of the non-linear relationships. This has been tried at the National Institute (see R. P. Byron, 'Initial attempts in econometric model building at NIESR' in Hilton and Heathfield (eds.), *The*

model there are eleven exogenous variables: exports, gross fixed investment and public authorities' consumption at constant prices; current grants to persons, forces' pay, net insurance contributions,[1] net transfers abroad and changes in hire purchase and bank debt at current prices; together with import prices, the indirect tax content of consumer prices, and time. These and the endogenous variables are interrelated either by behavioural relationships as described in earlier chapters, or by national income accounting or other identities, which can be shown schematically as follows:[2]

Behavioural equations

$$\begin{aligned}
&\mathit{IRSE} &&= \mathrm{f}(\mathrm{GDP}, \mathit{IRSE}_{-1})\\
&\mathit{DNI} &&= \mathrm{f}(\mathrm{GDP}, \mathit{DNI}_{-1})\\
&\mathit{WS} &&= \mathrm{f}(\mathrm{GDP}, \mathit{WS}_{-1}, \mathbf{TIM})\\
&\mathit{TAXWS} &&= \mathrm{f}(\mathit{WS}, \mathbf{TIM})\\
&\mathit{TAXO} &&= \mathrm{f}(\mathit{IRSE}, \mathit{DNI})\\
&\mathrm{CEND} &&= \mathrm{f}(\mathrm{RDW}, \mathrm{RDO}, \mathrm{CEND}_{-1})\\
&\mathrm{CPIFC} &&= \mathrm{f}(\mathit{WS}, \mathrm{GDP}, \mathbf{MP}, \mathrm{CPIFC}_{-1})\\
&\mathrm{FCA} &&= \mathrm{f}(\mathrm{CE})\\
&\mathrm{S} &&= \mathrm{f}(\mathrm{GDP}, \mathrm{TFS}, \mathrm{FCA}, \mathrm{S}_{-1})\\
&\mathrm{IMP} &&= \mathrm{f}(\mathrm{INV}, \mathrm{TFS})
\end{aligned}$$

Identities

$$\begin{aligned}
&\mathrm{CPI} &&= \alpha\,\mathrm{CPIFC} + \beta\mathbf{T}\\
&\mathrm{RDW} &&= (\mathit{WS} + \boldsymbol{FP} + \boldsymbol{NI} + \gamma\boldsymbol{CG} - \mathit{TAXWS})\,/\,\mathrm{CPI}\\
&\mathrm{RDO} &&= (\mathit{IRSE} + \mathit{DNI} - \boldsymbol{NTA} - \mathit{TAXO})\,/\,\mathrm{CPI}\\
&\mathrm{CE} &&= \mathrm{CEND} + (\boldsymbol{\Delta CR})\,/\,\mathrm{CPI}\\
&\mathrm{TFS} &&= \mathrm{CE} + \mathbf{PAC} + \mathbf{GFI} + \mathbf{EX}\\
&\mathrm{INV} &&= \mathrm{S} - \mathrm{S}_{-1}\\
&\mathrm{GDP} &&= \mathrm{TFS} + \mathrm{INV} - \mathrm{IMP} - \mathrm{FCA}
\end{aligned}$$

The formal model thus comprises ten behavioural equations and seven identities.

There is, however, an important complication. Each behavioural equation provides calculated values for the past which differ, quarter by quarter, from the actual values. These equation errors are presumed, statistically, to be distributed at random about a mean of zero. However, the reduction of

---

Econometric Study of the United Kingdom) but the heroic assumptions implicit in linearising, for example the relation between values, volumes and prices, make it difficult to accept. The main purpose of the work described by Byron was to enable simultaneous estimation to be used, rather than to ease the algebraic solution of the model.

[1] Employers' contributions to private pension schemes less employees' contributions to National Insurance, etc., see p. 54.

[2] With the standard notation (see p. viii), current-price values are in italics and exogenous variables are in bold type.

enormously complex reality to a set of very simplified aggregate relationships necessarily means that discrepancies between actual and estimated values of a variable may not simply be random errors, produced for example by inaccurate recording of actual values, but may reflect the influences of other factors affecting the variable which have been left out of the specified relationship. This has important implications for the use of the model in forecasting. For it may be the case that such a factor, not included in the specified relationship, is expected to have a noticeable influence on the variable in the future. For example, it might be believed that the pursuit of a very stringent monetary policy (which did not operate in the past and whose effects thus cannot be objectively estimated by regression analysis) will cause stockbuilding to be lower in the future than would be expected from the behavioural relationship included in the model. In that case, the best forecast would be obtained by assuming that the future errors in the stockbuilding function will show random fluctuations not about a zero mean but about a negative mean. Since random fluctuations by their nature cannot be predicted, this implies making an exogenous adjustment to the relationship for the forecast period – in effect adjusting the intercept term and specifying different values for each quarter of the forecast.

The reasons for, and the shape of, such intercept adjustments will vary widely. The reasons for making an adjustment may range from the powerful and easily quantifiable assumption that exports delayed by a dock strike in the current quarter will be shipped out in the course of the next quarter with equal and opposite effects on stockbuilding, to a much vaguer belief about a relationship which has, say, underpredicted consumption over several recent quarters. In the latter case, where a gradual return to predicting correctly is assumed, the intercept adjustment required will return towards zero; if the assumption is that a constant underprediction will continue, the intercept adjustment will remain constant; if the underprediction is assumed to be growing, the rate of change being underpredicted, the intercept adjustment will grow over time.

In extreme cases, where a relationship has provided calculated values for the recent past which have diverged by a wide margin from the actual values, the relationship may have to be rejected altogether and an alternative explanatory hypothesis investigated. This has happened for example in the case of average earnings (see chapter 5 above). In less extreme cases there may be room for a good deal of dispute as to why discrepancies have emerged and hence as to the intercept adjustment which should reasonably be made for the future. The paradigm case is that in which a new factor is thought to be influencing a relationship: there is, since the influence is a new one, no means of measuring its effect over the past. For example, wages and salaries have been rising more rapidly in the very recent past than would have been expected from established relationships with the pressure of demand. Possible new influences include the abnormal rise in consumer prices induced by the effect of devaluation on the prices of imported goods and the additional indirect taxation imposed as part of the devaluation strategy, reaction to the ending of incomes policy, and awareness by negotiators of inflation as a continuing aspect of the environment. Which hypothesis is believed will have an important influence on the intercept adjustment to be projected. The reaction to the devaluation-induced price rise will be a once-for-all effect, with earnings returning to a more normal rate of increase in time, though at a higher level than would otherwise have been expected. Adjustment to an inflationary environment, however, implies a continuing faster rate of increase, with the level of wages and salaries growing progressively higher than would otherwise have been expected. The adjustment to the ending of incomes policy might be more complex, with the level of earnings falling below the calculated value during the operation of the policy, rising above it in compensation after the ending of restraint and ultimately returning to the expected level. In the cases of other behavioural relationships it is easy to think of plausible ways in which current and future experience may differ from the average experience of the last ten or fifteen years over which the relationships were fitted.

To the eleven exogenous variables given above must therefore be added ten more – the intercept adjustment terms corresponding to the ten behavioural equations.[1] One version of the model is given in full in appendix II.

SOLUTION OF THE MODEL

Solution of the model on a computer proceeds quarter by quarter. This point is important, for it means that, in any given quarter, lagged values even of endogenous variables which appear in the behavioural equations can be treated as predetermined as well as the values of exogenous variables.

None of the set of behavioural equations depends on predetermined values only, so the whole model has to be solved simultaneously. The method employed in the solution programme is the Gauss-Seidel technique – an iteration procedure which solves the equations in sequence. A set of trial values for the unknown (non-predetermined) variables is chosen. In the first equation, the value of the dependent variable is calculated using these trial values for any non-predetermined value on the right-hand side. This solution value is then adjusted to form a new solution by a multiple of the difference between the trial value and the first solution value. The adjusted solution value so found is then used in conjunction with the remain-

[1] It might seem more appropriate in many of these cases to alter parameters in the relevant equations. This is easily done; in the short-term, however, it makes little difference which method is used and it is computationally more convenient to use intercept adjustments.

ing trial and predetermined values to find a first solution of the second equation, and so on. In all subsequent equations, the corrections made to the values of earlier variables are used in calculating the first solution value.[1] When the full set of adjusted solution values has been generated a convergence test is applied. If, in any equation, the difference between the initial trial value and the adjusted solution is greater than a designated amount, convergence is deemed not to have been achieved, and the whole process begins again using the adjusted solutions as the new trial values.

Algebraically, we have a set of n simultaneously determined variables:

(8.1) $x_i; \quad i = 1 \text{ to } n,$

and a set of m predetermined variables:

(8.2) $y_j; \quad j = 1 \text{ to } m,$

where

$$
\begin{aligned}
(8.3)\quad x_1 &= f_1(x_i, y_j); \quad i = 2 \text{ to } n, \quad j = 1 \text{ to } m,\\
x_2 &= f_2(x_i, y_j); \quad i = 1, 3 \text{ to } n, \; j = 1 \text{ to } m,\\
&\cdot\\
&\cdot\\
x_n &= f_n(x_i, y_j); \quad i = 1 \text{ to } n-1, j = 1 \text{ to } m.
\end{aligned}
$$

First we assume a set of trial values for the x_i, say x_i^o. Then we can calculate the solutions to successive equations as:

$$
\begin{aligned}
(8.4)\quad x_i' = f_i(x_k'', x_h^o, y_j); \quad i &= 1 \text{ to } n,\\
k &= 1 \text{ to } i-1,\\
h &= i+1 \text{ to } n,\\
j &= 1 \text{ to } m,
\end{aligned}
$$

where x_k'' is the adjusted solution for x_k (see 8.6 below).
In each case, the error is formed as:

(8.5) $e_i' = x_i' - x_i^o,$

and the adjusted solution x_i'' is

(8.6) $x_i'' = x_i' - a s_i e_i',$

where a is the given adjustment factor and

$$s_i = +1 \text{ if } \frac{\partial e_i'}{\partial x_i^o} \geqslant 0, \; -1 \text{ otherwise.}$$

That is, s_i indicates the direction of the change to be made to the solution to reduce the residual error, depending on the partial derivative of the error in the i-th equation with respect to the i-th variable evaluated using the initial trial values.

[1] It might seem simpler to calculate first solution values for *all* the equations and proceed in this way (the Jacobi method), but the Gauss-Seidel method tends, in practice, to produce more rapid convergence. For a description of these and other solution methods, see Charles C. Holt *et al.*, *Program Simulate II – a user's and programmer's manual*, Madison, Social Systems Research Institute, University of Wisconsin, 1967.

Convergence is achieved if and only if

(8.7) All $\left| x_i^{p+1} - x_i^{p} \right| \leqslant \delta$,

where x_i^{p+1} is the solution of the i-th equation after $p+1$ iterations and δ is a given small quantity.

Divergence is prevented by limiting the number of iterations to a given number N; this also has the advantage of stopping a very slow convergence. In the programme developed in connection with the National Institute model, α is taken as 1·0, δ as 0·01 per cent and N as 40.

Having reached convergence for the first quarter, the procedure is repeated for subsequent quarters one by one.

SIMULATION OF THE PAST

The model as a whole can be tested against the past to see whether it produces paths for the endogenous variables – incomes, consumers' expenditure, stockbuilding, output and so on – which follow closely the actual paths taken by these variables.

The actual values of the exogenous variables – exports, public consumption, fixed investment and so on – are fed in. This test does not provide a guide to the forecasting ability of the whole framework used at the National Institute, but only to the model's ability to predict the endogenous variables given accurate paths for the exogenous variables.

The results are shown in charts 4A–F. It will be seen that over the period 1958–69, the levels of the major endogenous variables were apparently simulated with a fairly high degree of accuracy.[1]

Consumers' expenditure appears to have been simulated reasonably well, with two exceptions. First, a rapid rate of growth was predicted for 1960–1, while in fact consumption grew rather slowly in this period. There does not appear to be any marked correlation of this error with those in incomes or prices, and it seems that it was the relationship between consumption and real incomes which failed in this period. There was in fact a marked recovery in personal savings between 1959/60 and 1960/1 (from 5·0 per cent to 8·1 per cent of personal disposable income) and it seems clear that this phenomenon resulted from a secular change in the short-run consumption function rather than from factors included in the specification of the function. The second period of poor simulation of consumption behaviour was 1962–3, when the rapid recovery of consumption occurred a little

[1] It is of course true that simulation over the period of estimation would be expected to be tolerably accurate, even though over the simulation period there is no correction for errors in the endogenous variables, that is errors are allowed to cumulate.

Chart 4. *Simulation of some variables of the model*

A: *Imports of goods and services*

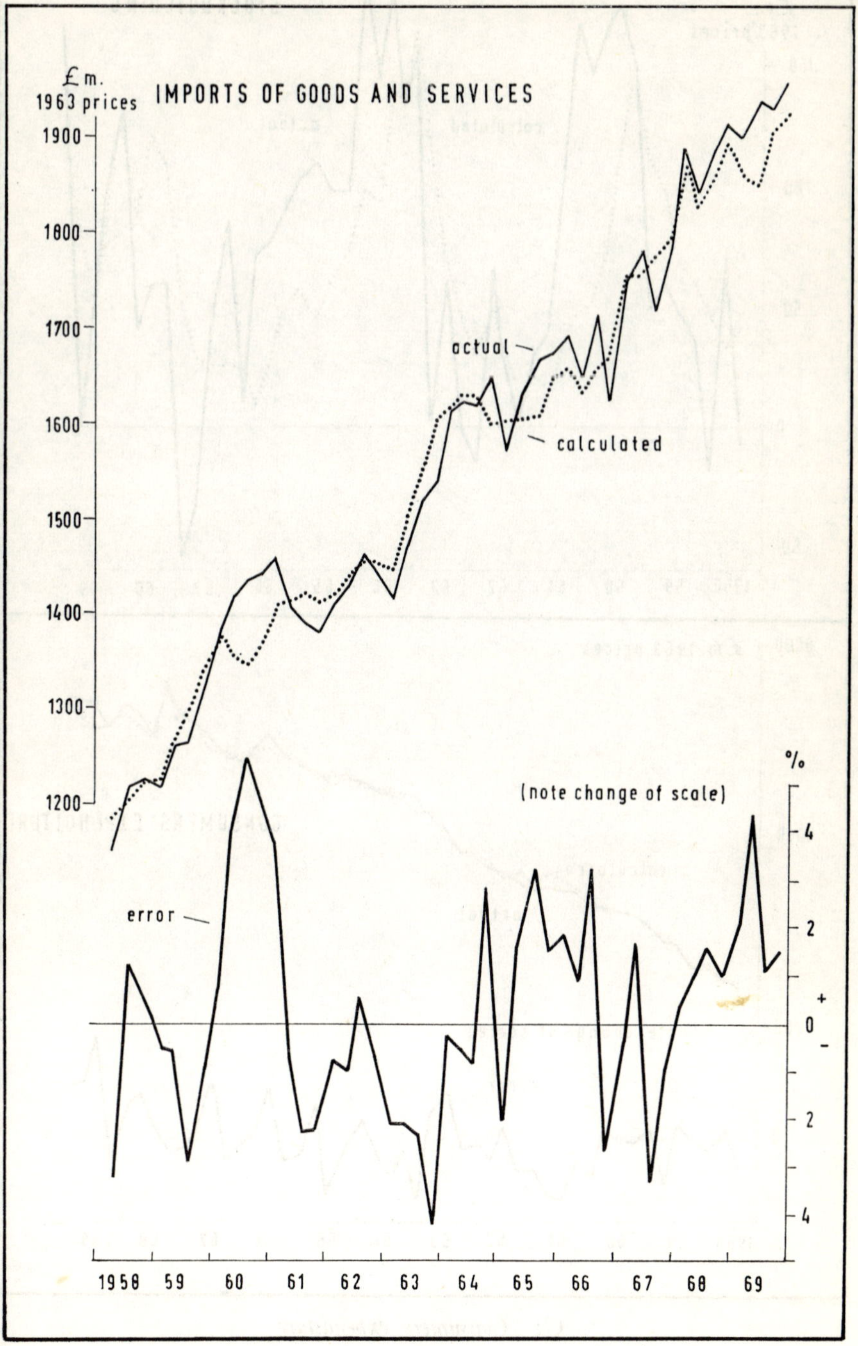

B: *Stockbuilding*

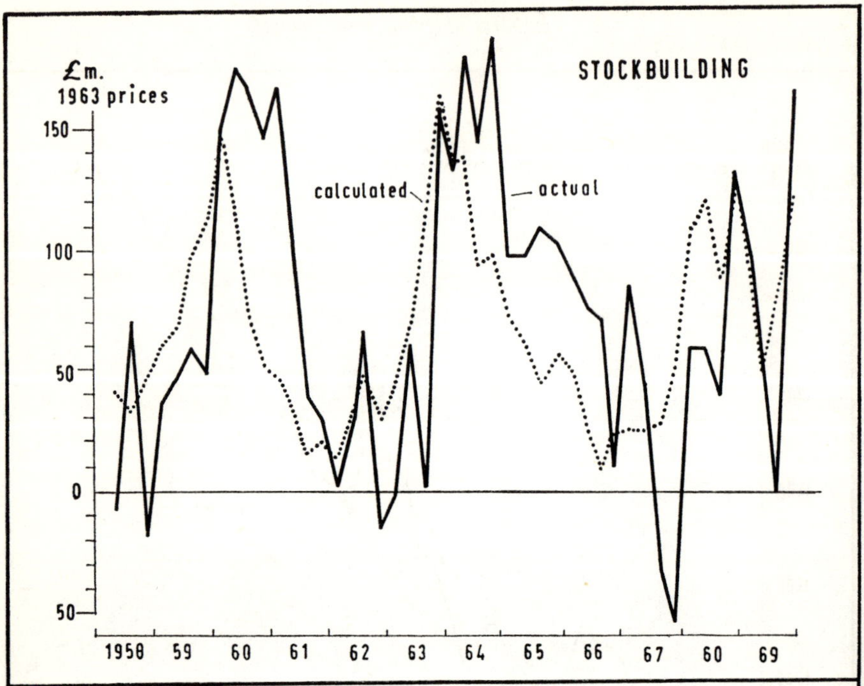

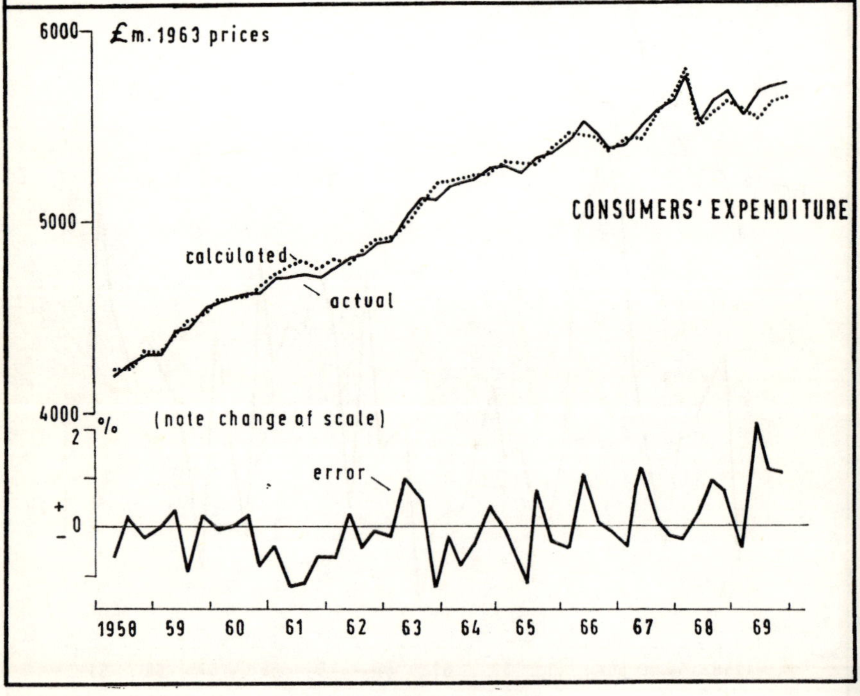

C: *Consumers' expenditure*

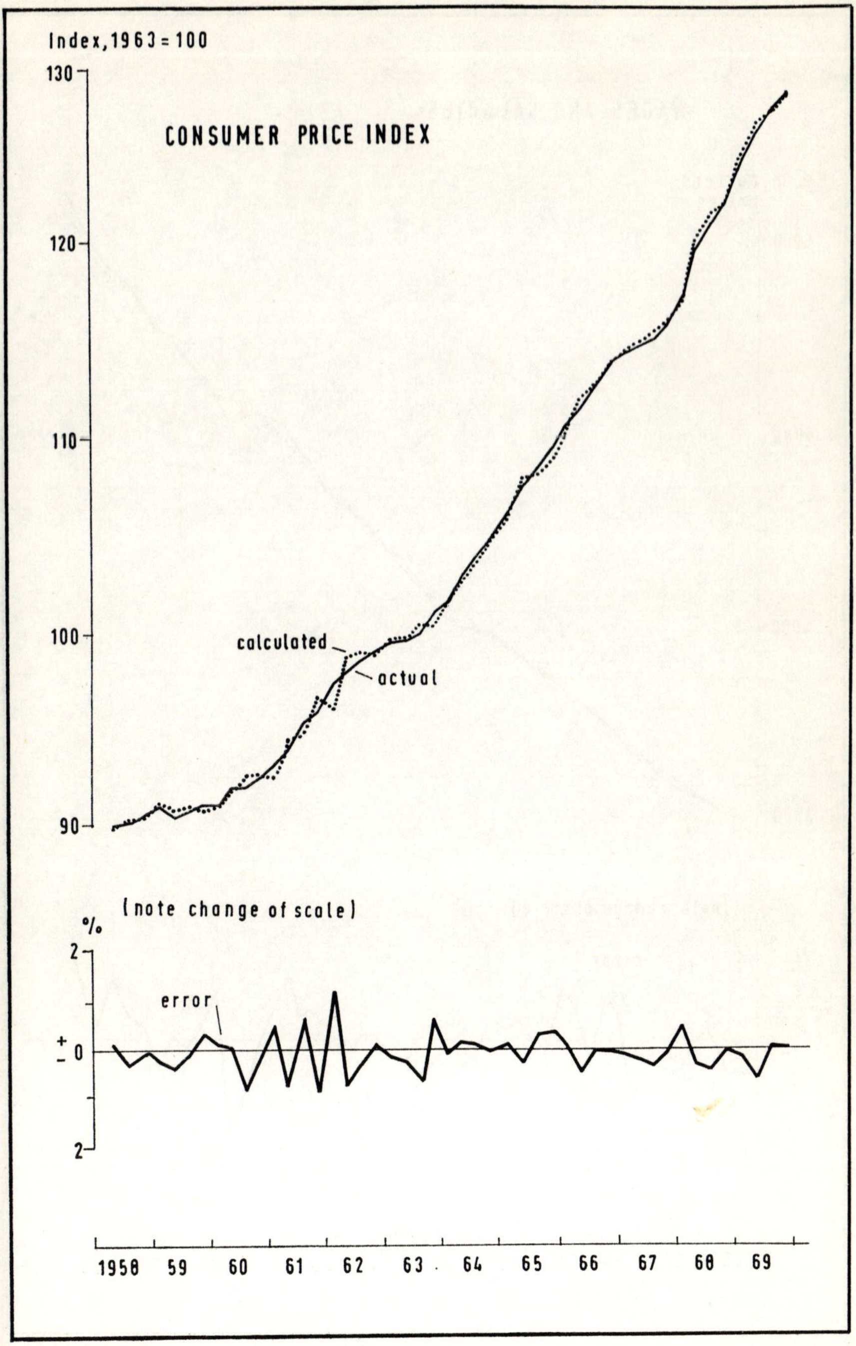
Index, 1963 = 100
130
120
110
100
90
CONSUMER PRICE INDEX
calculated
actual
(note change of scale)
%
2
± 0
2
error
1958
59
60
61
62
63
64
65
66
67
68
69

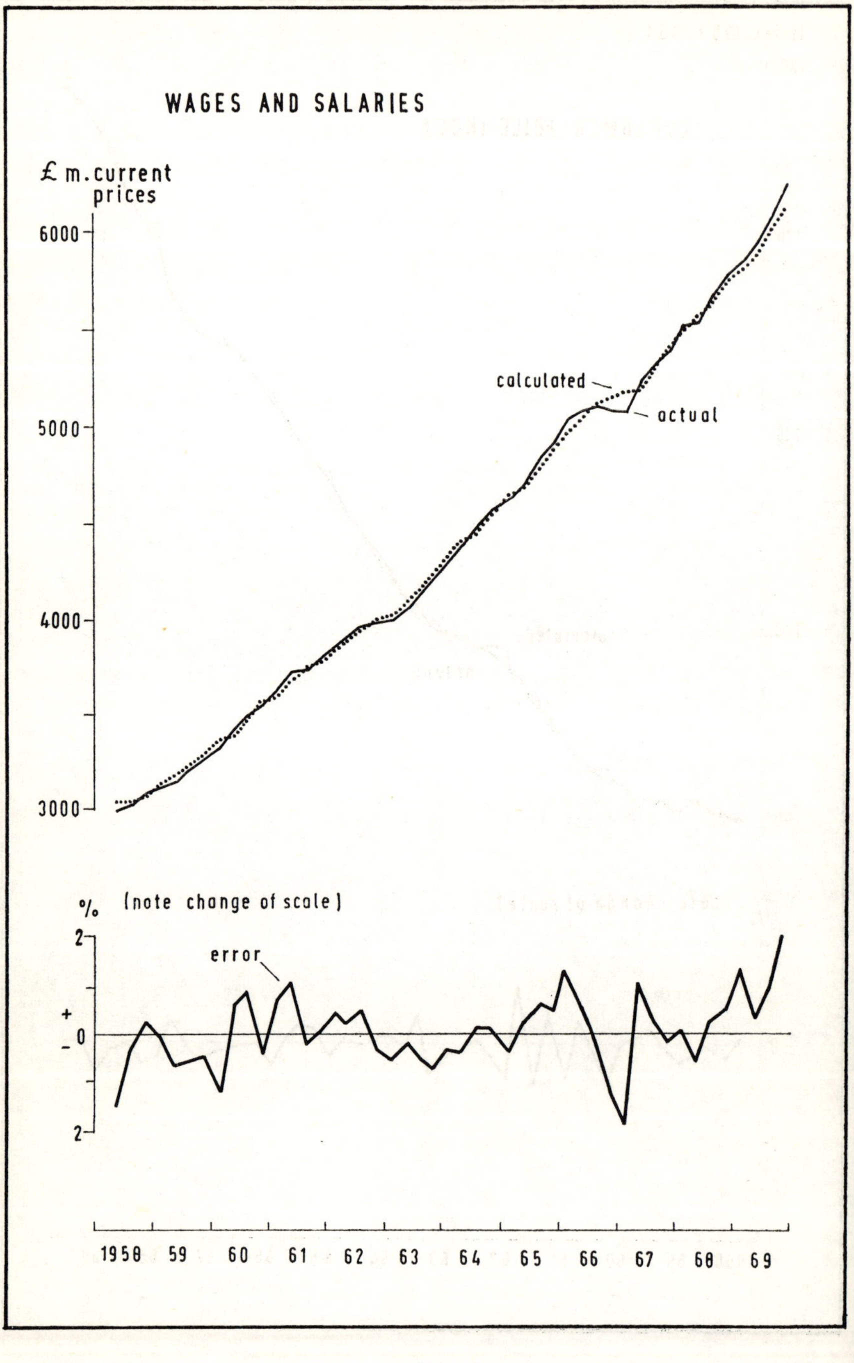
WAGES AND SALARIES
£ m. current prices
6000
5000
4000
3000
calculated
actual
% (note change of scale)
2
+
0
-
2
error
1958
59
60
61
62
63
64
65
66
67
68
69

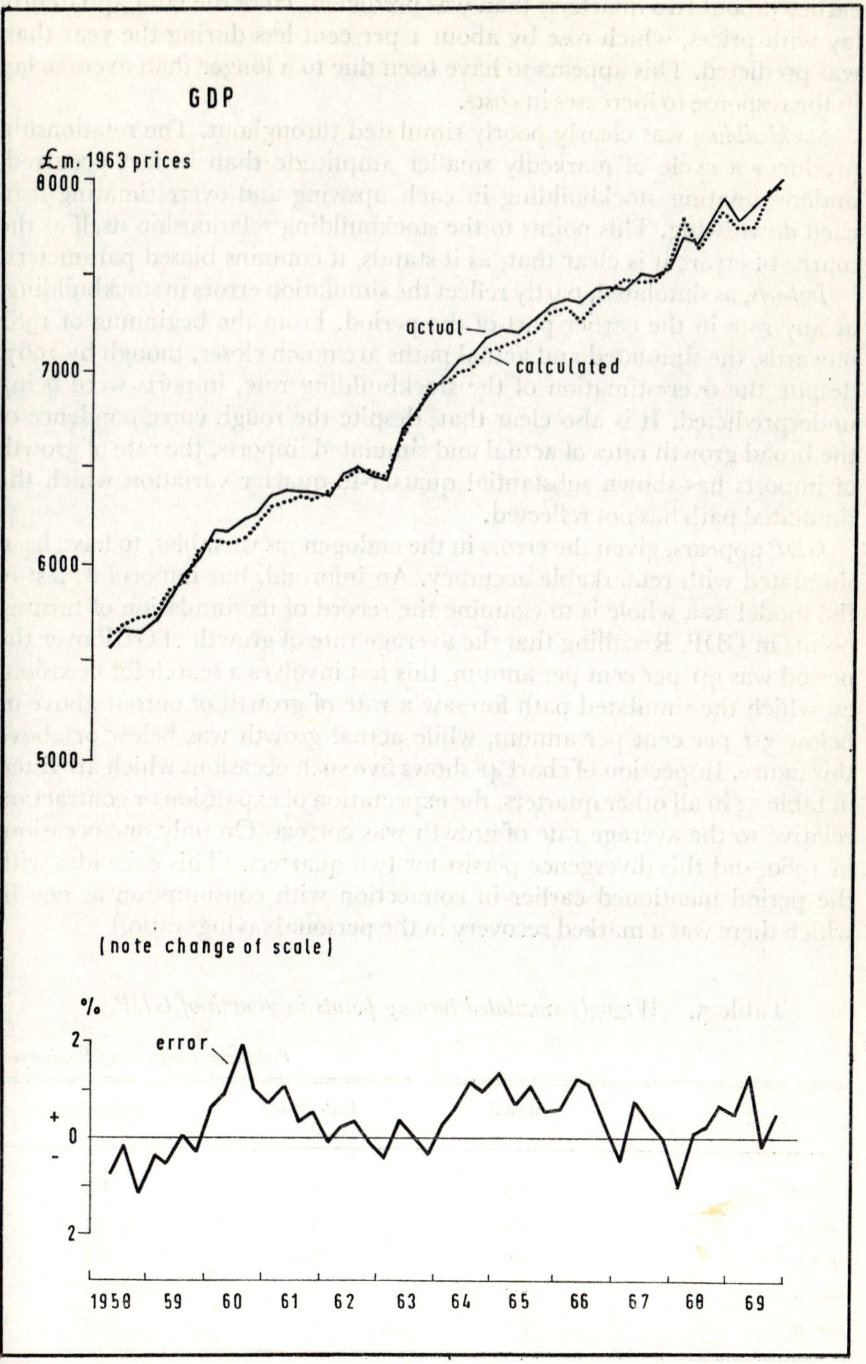
GDP
£m. 1963 prices
8000
7000
6000
5000
actual
calculated
(note change of scale)
%
2
error
+
0
-
2
1958
59
60
61
62
63
64
65
66
67
68
69

earlier (about two quarters) than was predicted. Here the fault apparently lay with prices, which rose by about 1 per cent less during the year than was predicted. This appears to have been due to a longer than average lag in the response to increases in costs.

Stockbuilding was clearly poorly simulated throughout. The relationship produces a cycle of markedly smaller amplitude than in fact occurred, underestimating stockbuilding in each upswing and overestimating it in each downswing. This points to the stockbuilding relationship itself as the source of error; it is clear that, as it stands, it contains biased parameters.

Imports, as simulated, partly reflect the simulation errors in stockbuilding, at any rate in the earlier part of the period. From the beginning of 1962 onwards, the simulated and actual paths are much closer, though by 1967, despite the overestimation of the stockbuilding rate, imports were being underpredicted. It is also clear that, despite the rough correspondence of the broad growth rates of actual and simulated imports, the rate of growth of imports has shown substantial quarter-to-quarter variation which the simulated path has not reflected.

GDP appears, given the errors in the endogenous variables, to have been simulated with remarkable accuracy. An informal, but important, test of the model as a whole is to examine the record of its simulation of turning points in GDP. Recalling that the average rate of growth of GDP over the period was 3·1 per cent per annum, this test involves a search for occasions on which the simulated path foresaw a rate of growth of output above or below 3·1 per cent per annum, while actual growth was below or above this figure. Inspection of chart 4F shows five such occasions which are listed in table 5; in all other quarters, the expectation of expansion or contraction relative to the average rate of growth was correct. On only one occasion, in 1960, did this divergence persist for two quarters. (This coincides with the period mentioned earlier in connection with consumption as one in which there was a marked recovery in the personal savings ratio.)

Table 5. *Wrongly simulated turning points in growth of GDP*

Percentage changes over following year

	Actual	Calculated	Difference
1959 IV	3·5	2·2	1·3
1960 III	2·3	4·7	−2·4
1960 IV	2·0	3·3	−1·3
1962 II	3·7	1·5	2·2
1966 II	2·0	3·5	−1·5

Table 6. *Correlation matrix of simulation errors*

	IRSE	*DNI*	*TAXO*	*WS*	*TAXWS*	CE	CPI	FCA	INV	IMP	GDP
IRSE	1·00										
DNI	0·11	1·00									
TAXO	0·28	0·59	1·00								
WS	0·55	0·44	0·31	1·00							
TAXWS	−0·11	0·20	0·04	0·45	1·00						
CE	0·70	0·18	0·12	0·70	0·05	1·00					
CPI	−0·48	−0·28	−0·20	−0·39	0·09	−0·66	1·00				
FCA	0·38	−0·29	−0·27	0·23	−0·03	0·55	−0·37	1·00			
INV	0·03	0·12	0·11	0·08	0·29	0·07	−0·15	0·16	1·00		
IMP	0·51	0·10	0·12	0·57	0·06	0·64	−0·48	0·48	0·44	1·00	
GDP	0·40	0·50	0·38	0·52	0·22	0·57	−0·56	−0·08	0·43	0·50	1·00

SYMBOLS: see p. viii.

The error correlation matrix is shown in table 6. *A priori* expectations about the sizes of these correlations are rather obscure because of the simultaneity of the model. For example, overprediction of consumers' expenditure is likely to lead to consequential overprediction of GDP: to this extent a positive correlation of the errors in the two would be expected. Equally, the overprediction of GDP should lead to an overprediction of consumption thus reinforcing the expectation of a positive correlation. But in the case of imports, overprediction should lead to underprediction of GDP and hence to a negative correlation, while underprediction of GDP should lead to underprediction of imports, suggesting a positive correlation of errors.

In some cases, it is possible to say with some conviction in which direction the causal link between correlated errors operates. For example, the high correlation between errors in consumers' expenditure and the factor cost adjustment suggests that some of the errors in the latter are caused by errors in the former, for that link is strong and direct, whereas the link between the factor cost adjustment and consumers' expenditure through GDP and incomes is both weak and in the opposite direction. But, in general, the error correlation matrix provides little information about the important sources of error in the model.

SHOCKS, LAGS AND MULTIPLIERS

The essential properties of the model can be summarised by describing the impact on the economy which it implies, given an exogenous change in one variable or another. There are three aspects of the behaviour of the model following such a change. First, there are direct leakages: an increase of £100 million in consumers' expenditure, for example, will automatically raise imports by £21 million and the factor cost adjustment by £31 million even before multiplier effects, leaving a direct stimulus to output of only £48 million. Secondly, there are multiplier (and accelerator) effects which, thirdly, are lagged: the stimulus to output will, for example, raise employment and earnings, thus reinforcing the initial stimulus to consumption. A direct stimulus of £100 million to GDP gives rise to secondary expansion such that total GDP reaches £150 million by the third and fourth quarters, but then drops back very nearly asymptotically (there is in fact a highly damped cycle) to about £140 million. Thus the implied GDP multiplier is about 1·4; convergence is virtually complete after twelve quarters.[1]

Table 7. *Effects on GDP of exogenous stimuli*

£ millions

Leakages	Direct effect on GDP	The multiplier	Secondary effect on GDP
+ 100 in:		+ 100 GDP in quarter:	
Consumers' expenditure	+48	1	143
Public authorities'		2	145
consumption	+79	3	150
Gross fixed investment	+79	4	151
Exports	+79	8	145
Stockbuilding	+68	12	140
Imports	−100	16	137
Factor cost adjustment	−100	∞	139

SOURCE: NIESR estimates.

Table 7 summarises these properties of the model. The very muted cyclical variation shown in the last column reflects the operation of the accelerator implicit in the stockbuilding function. (It will be recalled that there is no fixed investment accelerator in the present form of the model; fixed investment is treated as wholly exogenous and thus invariant with respect to shocks of the kind under discussion. Clearly, an important next step in simulation studies will be to incorporate an accelerator element.)

[1] These characteristics can be used to trace the indirect effects of tax changes when the direct (revenue) effect is known. See also J. R. Shepherd and M. J. C. Surrey, 'The short-term effects of tax changes', *National Institute Economic Review*, No. 46, November 1968.

CHAPTER 9

SHORT-TERM ECONOMIC FORECASTING

The preceding chapters have described the analysis of the economy with an emphasis on the formation and testing of relatively simple hypotheses to explain the broad changes which have taken place over the last ten or fifteen years. The use of these relationships in economic forecasting is far from mechanical. The main reason for this is that it is rarely possible to presume with any confidence that relationships which have fitted well to the experience of a period of ten to fifteen years will continue to fit well in the future. In some cases, a relationship may have ceased to fit satisfactorily in the most recent year or two; the problem then is to try to identify the reasons for the apparent departure from the more stable relationship of earlier years, and to gauge the likely influence of such identified factors over the forecast period. In other cases, even though the relationship still fits well in the very recent past, there may be good reason to suppose that special distorting factors will arise during the forecast period; the problem is then one of making what appears to be 'reasonable' allowance for such factors.

Earlier chapters may thus have given an over precise impression of the way in which an economic forecast is compiled. The aim of the present chapter is to redress the balance by describing briefly the steps taken to produce a forecast of the kind published in the *National Institute Economic Review* every three months. The whole exercise involves a staff of some fifteen economists and takes something like a month.

FORECASTING THE PAST

The first stage is to get as clear a picture as possible of the very recent past and the current situation, for which official statistics are not yet available. The lags with which the statistics appear vary widely, from unemployment (about ten days after the day of the count) to employment (up to nine months later). Complete quarterly figures for the balance of payments appear some ten weeks after the end of the quarter to which they relate, and for the domestic economy the lag is about fourteen weeks. Thus for a forecast to appear, for example, in the February *Review*, the main work has to be completed early in February, at which time national accounts up to and including the third quarter of the previous year are available. For the fourth quarter of that year, a large number of monthly indicators have appeared – industrial production, retail sales, unemployment, trade figures, and so on – and these are used to 'mock up' estimates of the national and balance of payments accounts. For the first quarter of the year in which the forecast is being made very little information is available, and such as there is is used to check the plausibility of a forecast 'from scratch' rather than to attempt an estimate of the national accounts.

On the domestic side, the most recent complete calendar quarter is only partially covered by monthly indicators. The volume of industrial production (and the unemployment figures) can be used to form a view about the level of total output (GDP). Of the expenditure components, consumers' expenditure can be estimated with some precision from the volume of retail sales, changes in hire purchase and bank lending, and registrations of cars. Exports of goods and services can be inferred from the trade figures and from the later volume index based on those figures, and the position is similar for imports. There is little evidence, however, on which to base estimates of private fixed investment and no evidence at all on public expenditure and stockbuilding. In practice, a view about public expenditure and private investment is based on the previous forecast, and stockbuilding is estimated partly on the basis of the stockbuilding function and partly as the residual required to make the net sum of expenditures equal to GDP.

On the balance of payments side, the trade figures give a reasonably precise picture of visible trade, and the monthly estimate of the *balance* of invisible trade made by the Central Statistical Office can be used.

Some of these relationships between quarterly national accounting aggregates and monthly indicators have been formalised. For GDP in relation to the quarter's industrial production figures, regression analysis gives:

$$(9.1)\quad GDP = \underset{(939)}{-10{,}874} + \underset{(209.4)}{3{,}736.5}\log_e P + \underset{(1.8)}{20.3}t$$

$$R^2 = 0.9975 \qquad SE = 30.9\ (0.45\%) \qquad DW = 2.13$$

where GDP = gross domestic product in £ millions at 1963 prices, quarterly and seasonally adjusted,

P = index of industrial production (1963 = 100) quarterly and seasonally adjusted

and the estimation period is 1959 I to 1968 IV.

This log-linear relationship implies that the share of industrial production in GDP is increasing over time.

For consumers' expenditure, the relationships for different parts are:[1]

$$(9.2)\quad CE^* = \underset{(329)}{2{,}467} + \underset{(3.2)}{23.2}\,TRS + \underset{(1.7)}{15.8}t$$

$$R^2 = 0.989 \qquad SE = 21.5 \qquad DW = 1.7$$

[1] These equations may be compared with those using a similar approach employed by the Central Statistical Office in producing preliminary estimates of consumers' expenditure (see *Economic Trends*, No. 187, May 1969).

(9.3) $$CE^{**} = -26{\cdot}5 + 2{\cdot}44\,NR + 2{\cdot}40t$$
$$\quad\quad\quad (0{\cdot}22) \quad\quad (0{\cdot}51)$$
$$R^2 = 0{\cdot}874 \qquad SE = 12{\cdot}9 \qquad DW = 2{\cdot}44$$

where CE* = consumers' expenditure other than on cars and motorcycles, in £ millions at 1963 prices,

CE** = consumers' expenditure on cars and motorcycles, in £ millions at 1963 prices,

TRS = index of the volume of total retail sales (1963 = 100),

NR = new registrations of cars and motorcycles (thousands),

all quarterly and seasonally adjusted,

and t = 0 in 1965 I.

The final formal equation used in estimating the latest quarter's consumer price index from the three months' retail price index is:

(9.4) $$CPI = 3{\cdot}27 + 0{\cdot}936\,RPI - 0{\cdot}74s_2$$
$$(0{\cdot}84) \quad (0{\cdot}007) \quad\quad (0{\cdot}1)$$
$$R^2 = 0{\cdot}9987 \qquad SE = 0{\cdot}265 \qquad DW = 1{\cdot}68$$

where *CPI* = deflator of consumers' expenditure (1963 = 100) quarterly and seasonally adjusted,

RPI = average of three months' retail price index for all items (January 1962 = 100), not seasonally adjusted,

and s_2 = second quarter seasonal dummy.

Although relationships of this kind can be time saving, they do no more than formalise the inevitable use of monthly indicators. The use of such relationships could be extended to cover imports and exports and, probably, wage and salary earnings; also to construct estimates when only one or two months' figures are available. But, as has already been mentioned, there are large areas of the national accounts where no monthly indicators exist, and 'forecasting the past' is likely to remain part of the forecaster's lot.

THE EXOGENOUS VARIABLES

The next step is to forecast those elements of the framework which are regarded as exogenous – that is, more or less unaffected by the outcome of the remainder of the forecasting exercise.[1] The first of these elements is *exports*.[2] The results of research into formal relationships determining exports have already been described. In practice, these relationships have not proved particularly satisfactory as forecasting tools, and they are employed more to

[1] Exogeneity thus may result either from the assumed absence of causal links with other variables, or because, even though such causal links are believed to exist, they have not been satisfactorily estimated.

[2] Export forecasting is also discussed in chapter 4.

check the plausibility of forecasts derived less formally. The first step in export forecasting is to form a view about the development of world trade. For the industrial countries of OECD, much use is made of the own-country forecasts of growth and imports made by other European research institutes and by United States commentators. The assumptions on which these forecasts rest are of course critically examined, and account is taken of developments since their appearance. Commentators' views also play a part in similar forecasts for the developed sterling area countries. For the remainder of the sterling area, some attempt is made to assess trends in their exports, and hence in their reserve positions, as a guide to their import demands.[1]

On the basis of the output and import forecasts for the rest of the world so derived, an aggregate view as to the likely rate of increase of world trade can be formed. The rate of increase of the value of United Kingdom exports is related directly, though informally, to world trade. As mentioned earlier, the chief characteristics of this relationship are that the British share in world trade has fallen steadily, and at a faster rate when world trade is expanding more rapidly.[2]

The resulting forecast of exports in current value terms is revalued to constant 1963 prices for the domestic output forecast, using a projection of export average values based on the likely evolution of home costs and other factors.[3]

The methods of forecasting *public sector expenditures* have been described in chapters 2 and 3. In practice, government plans and projections, particularly of investment expenditures, are examined critically, programme by programme, in the light of a host of factors whose influence has not been formally assessed. These include the likely rates of change of non-public sector demands and of interest rates, and supply considerations.

Private fixed investment falls into several categories – investment in dwellings, investment by manufacturing industry, and investment by other private industry. Investment in dwellings, notwithstanding the relationships described in chapter 3, is forecast informally, taking particular

[1] These assessments, and the view of world trade to which they give rise, are regularly reported in the *National Institute Economic Review* in the chapter on 'The World Economy'.

[2] See chapter 4, pp. 42–3.

[3] See chapter 4. None of the aggregate export or import functions, and few of the disaggregated relations used in forecasting, include terms which measure the effect of changes in relative prices or in alternative measures of competitiveness. Econometric research has been disappointing in its failure to locate significant and plausible values of price elasticities in international trade. Consequently the likely effects of changes in competitiveness are introduced into a forecast either implicitly, as for example one of the causes of a continual decline in the British share of world trade, or explicitly but in an informal way, by allowing for price changes after a forecast has been derived formally from an equation. The effects of devaluation have been treated in both these ways. For a comparison of the forecasts made in November 1967 and the outcome of devaluation as seen in early 1970, see G. D. N. Worswick, 'Trade and Payments' in Sir Alec Cairncross (ed.), *Britain's Economic Prospects Reconsidered*, London, Allen and Unwin, 1971.

account of recent levels of starts (for investment in the immediate future) and of the likely mortgage situation; the surveys of builders' intentions are also an important overall influence. The forecast of investment by manufacturing industry is, in contrast, based to a much greater degree on the kind of relationship described in chapter 3. Even so, there are important sources of information which may be used to modify the results produced by the equation: the government surveys of investment intentions have already been mentioned; other surveys of business intentions are produced by the Confederation of British Industry and, with a shorter-term outlook, the monthly surveys of business opinion conducted by the *Financial Times* are a useful indicator of willingness to invest.[1] Other private investment – by the distributive, financial and other services sectors – is forecast informally, mainly with reference to the government's survey of investment intentions.

These three kinds of expenditure – exports, public expenditure and private fixed investment – are the exogenous elements on the expenditure side of the forecast. On the income side, the main elements which have to be forecast without reference to formal relationships are current grants to persons, National Insurance contributions, and the change in personal credit.

The forecast levels of both current grants and National Insurance contributions are heavily dependent on changes in rates expected to be introduced by the government. The main forecasting problem is thus to take account of government announcements and to gauge their effect, mainly by reference to the effects of changes made in the past.[2] Apart from such changes, the forecast is based on the projection of rates of increase observed over past periods. The forecast as a whole is normally conducted on the basis of 'unchanged policies' since, as a guide to policy decisions, the purpose is to provide a reference point which is conveniently taken as that in which no policy initiative is assumed.[3] Thus, in the absence of an announced government commitment to change rates of benefit or contributions, it is specifically assumed that existing rates will continue.

This assumption also applies to changes in the regulations governing hire-purchase, which are never announced beforehand, so that the forecast is invariably based on the assumption of the existing terms continuing. Government policy in respect of the supply of credit may, however, pose problems about the exact meaning of 'unchanged policies'. In recent years,

[1] Such surveys cover a wider field than investment intentions and are, in general, an important source of critical appraisal of other aspects of the economic forecasts – prices, stockbuilding, employment, and so on. As the forecast period lengthens, however, the availability of such material decreases.

[2] In some cases, the government may announce the expected revenue cost or yield of such changes and a direct forecast can then be made.

[3] See further, Introduction, p. 3.

government-imposed ceilings on levels of lending by banks and finance houses have had some effect in moderating the rates of increase of personal credit which might otherwise have been expected. It thus has become a matter for debate whether, when a ceiling for the current year is in operation, 'unchanged policies' implies that the ceiling will lapse at the end of the current period, or that it will continue indefinitely. In practice, the assumption on which the forecast is made is based on an appraisal of the likely approach of the government and is made explicit in presenting the forecast.[1] Apart from these considerations, credit is normally assumed to expand at a rate similar to that experienced in past periods, after making allowance for any remaining effects of recent changes in regulations (see above, chapter 8).

Less important exogenous elements of the income forecasts are forces' pay (projected by extrapolation, together with any specific information provided by the government) and net transfers abroad (projected by extrapolation in the light of other balance of payments developments).

The list of exogenous variables of which forecasts are required (see above, page 72) is completed by import prices (see chapter 4) and the indirect tax content of consumer prices. The latter is projected forward at the current level (given the assumption of unchanged policies and hence unchanged tax rates) after allowing for the delayed effects of any recent changes in indirect tax rates.

USING THE MODEL

The next stage in the preparation of a forecast is to examine each of the relationships which comprise the model in order to assess its behaviour over the recent past – generally, about the last two years. This calculation is a purely mechanical process: given actual values for the exogenous and other independent variables in each relationship, we ask what was the run of calculated values of each endogenous variable, and how this run differed from the run of actual values. To take an example, suppose that actual and calculated values of consumers' expenditure differed by the following amounts in the eight quarters preceding a forecast made in February of year t:

	Year t–2				*Year t–1*			
	I	II	III	IV	I	II	III	IV
Actual *less* calculated consumers' expenditure in £ millions at 1963 prices	25	15	–5	20	120	–60	30	60

[1] Another factor with some influence on the forecast of consumer credit is the level of interest rates. Here, a broad view about likely developments is taken; again, the assumption is made explicit in presenting the forecast.

Then the assessment might run like this: over the whole period, the average residual was + £25 million – a little less if the final quarter (based on an estimate of consumption, not on national accounts figures) is excluded. The first two quarters of the second year were apparently distorted by a switch of purchasing into the first quarter, perhaps in anticipation of a 'tough' budget. The 'underlying' residual might have been + £30 million in each case, with £90 million of anticipatory buying. In that case, there was some growth in the residual from an average of about £15 million in the first year to £30 million in the first three quarters of the second year, and to an estimated £60 million in the final quarter.

At what values should this residual be projected over the forecast period? Purely on grounds of extrapolation, a further slow rise might be forecast. But if, for example, the increase of consumption above the levels expected from the 'normal' relation to income represents the reluctance of consumers to slow down their rate of improvement of living standards even when incomes are rising more slowly than usual, then future behaviour depends on the rate of increase of incomes. If incomes continue to rise slowly, the residual may continue to grow. But if incomes rise more rapidly, the residual may vanish as the consumption–income relationship returns to normal, or even reverse sign as consumers make up for lost savings in the period when their consumption was taking a proportion of income greater than normal.

Even when the general shape of the discrepancy to be projected is settled, the problem of the starting point remains. At its face value, the final residual of £60 million suggests a high starting level. But there is a considerable margin of error attached to the estimate of consumption in that quarter, and the jump from the levels of the discrepancy earlier in the year might be partially discounted; the 'underlying' starting point might, for example, be taken as £40 million.[1]

One factor which might distort the 'normal' relationship embodied in the consumption function of the model has already been mentioned – the possibility of reaction to an unusually extended period of restraint on real incomes. There are many other candidates whose influence has in the past been too diffuse or too uniform to be picked up in empirical analysis, but which can plausibly be argued to be having a noticeable effect on current behaviour – the influence of government monetary policy, of unrecorded credit transactions or of unusually rapid price inflation, for example. The 'art' of forecasting lies to a considerable extent in the formulation of such hypotheses and their expression in quantitative form when, by

[1] A forecaster beginning to forecast a year earlier would be becoming aware of the very sharp increase in the consumption residual in that quarter, but, lacking the evidence of the second quarter, he would not necessarily realise that an anticipatory spurt was taking place. His problems in forecasting the residual for the remainder of the year would clearly be formidable.

definition, they have not proved amenable to empirical analysis in past periods.[1]

In some cases, economic indicators can provide helpful evidence in discussions of this kind. In the case of consumption, for example, data on the growth of mail-order credit trading may help to decide whether this could have been an important factor in the relationship between changes in credit and changes in incomes and consumption in a period of restraint on other forms of credit. Data from surveys of business opinion may indicate a markedly different rate of change in for instance wage costs or stock-building from that predicted using the equation. In such cases, a reconciliation may be achieved by including a residual path in the model relationship such that the resulting forecast comes closer to that suggested, informally, by the survey data. A path of residuals over the forecast period for each relationship is thus specified and a complete forecast can then be generated (see also chapter 8 above).

This forecast can then be examined as a whole in the light of its plausibility as a general picture of the likely behaviour of the economy. It may be that the predicted path of imports, say, despite the apparent plausibility of the discrepancies included in the import function, simply does not square with the rough expectations formed by the balance of payments analysis.[2] In this case, the conflict may be resolved by re-examining the import discrepancy and re-solving the model to generate a revised forecast.[3] Forecasts can also be prepared on alternative assumptions – of different rates of growth of wages and salaries, for example – simply by feeding two different sets of residuals into the wage and salary equation.

THE BALANCE OF PAYMENTS

The aim of the balance of payments account is to summarise all the transactions taking place between residents of the United Kingdom and non-residents. Such transactions include the sale of domestically produced goods and services (exporting), the purchase of goods and services produced abroad (importing), receipts of income from economic activities pursued

[1] The problem of forecasting discrepancies between actual and calculated values also arises, of course, when formal relationships are used in predicting exogenous variables outside the model – exports and manufacturing investment, for example; then the same kinds of consideration apply as those discussed here. Within the model, the emergence of discrepancies may suggest that the structure of the model needs revision.

[2] The basic forecast of imports produced by the model is determined solely by factors affecting the domestic economy. A different view can thus be taken by the balance of payments analysts, who can point, for example, to supply factors in the rest of the world of which no account is taken in the formal relationship.

[3] Similar conflicts can arise between forecasts of supposedly 'exogenous' elements and of the remainder. The model makes it possible quickly to generate a new forecast on a revised projection of the exogenous variable in question.

abroad by United Kingdom residents (income from abroad) and, conversely, income paid abroad. These transactions, directly following from economic activity of one sort or another, are reflected in the national expenditure accounts. Other kinds of transaction which have a less clear-cut relation to economic activity are, for example, international transfer payments, such as government aid to developing countries or migrants' remittances home.

All these transactions together make up the *current account*. *Capital flows* comprise inter-government loans and other government long-term capital transactions, private investment, trade credits, changes in banks' other claims and liabilities, and so on. In some periods there are also special official monetary transactions (in 1970, for example, the receipt of Special Drawing Rights on the International Monetary Fund and the payment of an additional subscription to the Fund) which, together with the balance on current account and the capital flows, make up the balance to be financed by changes in the reserves or by receipts and repayments of international assistance, including drawings on the International Monetary Fund. Each transaction involves in principle both a credit and a debit. But in practice it is not always possible to match credits and debits precisely, and a balancing item is required to offset the errors and omissions which arise.[1] Table 8 summarises the balance of payments account for 1970.

Accounts have been given of the methods of analysis and forecasting used in connection with the main components of the current balance – imports and exports.[2] Exports of goods are initially analysed on the basis of the trade accounts and in value terms. But as the statistical basis of the monthly trade accounts does not correspond exactly with the conceptual basis on which the balance of payments is constructed, some adjustments are necessary to translate the initial projection into a corresponding forecast of exports in the balance of payments.[3]

On the import side there are no problems of adjustment, since in our procedure the coverage of the initial forecast coincides with that used in the balance of payments accounts, but the basic constant-price forecast of imports of goods and services must be split between goods and services, and revalued to current prices. The forecast for imports of goods at constant

[1] For a fuller description of balance of payments accounting see *National Accounts Statistics – Sources and Methods*, chapter 15.

[2] See chapter 4.

[3] Specifically, the trade accounts record the value of goods leaving the geographical territory of the United Kingdom, while the balance of payments is concerned with the value of goods leaving United Kingdom ownership. The main adjustments are the exclusion of returned goods and the inclusion of second-hand ships and aircraft, letter post, imports of tin for the buffer stock established under the International Tin Agreement, and certain other items. These adjustments are forecast by interpreting recent trends in the light of particular circumstances in, for example, the second-hand ship market or the buffer stock of tin.

Table 8. *The balance of payments in 1970*

£ millions

Imports of goods and services	−10,529
Exports of goods and services	+10,869
Net income from abroad	+532
Net transfers abroad	−241
Balance on current account	+631
Government long-term capital	−205
Private investment	−88
Trade credit	−292
Other liabilities in sterling area currencies	+652
Other transactions of UK banks in non-sterling area currencies	+313
Miscellaneous capital flows	+119
Total capital flows	+499
Balancing item	+157
Special official monetary transactions	+133
Balance of above items	+1,420
Financed by:	
Net repayment of international assistance	−1,295
Additions to reserves	−125

SOURCE: *Economic Trends*, No. 211, March 1971.

prices is obtained by deducting from the forecast of total imports a forecast of imports of services at constant prices (see below). The goods forecast is then converted to a current-price basis using the forecast of import unit values (see chapter 4, pages 48–9).[1]

The invisible items in the current account comprise imports and exports of services (government transactions, shipping, civil aviation, travel and miscellaneous), net property income and transfers. The forecasts of all these items rely heavily on the extrapolation of trends in the recent past although allowance is made (in no very precise or systematic way) for a number of factors which may influence future movements. Official policy statements, especially on military establishments overseas, may affect the forecast of government transactions; prospects for world and United King-

[1] It is usually assumed that the average value index used in the balance of payments account will move broadly in line with the unit value index, but, since the latter includes freight and insurance costs which are excluded from the balance of payments valuation of imports, allowance must be made for any likelihood of atypical movements in ocean freight rates.

dom trade bear on the forecast of shipping earnings, and travel restrictions and the level of personal incomes will affect the balance of travel expenditures. In the case of imports of services, a constant-price series is also needed (see above). Again, the extrapolation of past trends is the main basis of the forecast, with allowance for such factors as the likely behaviour of freight rates.

Net property income tends to fluctuate erratically and is correspondingly difficult to predict over short periods. The occasional deferment of annual interest payments on the North American loan is one identifiable factor which clearly contributes to the irregularity; another is changes in Bank rate, which have a quite significant effect on net interest payments on sterling balances (probably of the order of £20 million in a full year for each 1 per cent change). On these factors a specific view can be taken for forecasting purposes, but it is harder to deal with other major sources of irregularity.[1]

Net transfers are a relatively stable item. A gradual increase in the deficit is usually projected, with the pace governed mainly by the official aid programme.

Because of their extreme volatility in the short-term, no attempt is now made at systematic forecasting of the various components of the capital account.

[1] Notably that caused by the rather unsatisfactory method of recording oil companies' earnings in the official statistics – on a cash flow basis, taking account, for example, of actual payments of (rather than accrued liability for) taxes overseas. Information is occasionally available on the likely timing of such tax payments, but it is usually practicable to allow only for the probable trend in net earnings in the light of the likely profitability of the oil industry and the general prospects for overseas economic expansion. Net earnings on other types of direct investment also depend on relative profit levels in this country and overseas; again, in practice, they are difficult to forecast other than by the projection of a plausible trend.

APPENDIX I

MEASURING NATIONAL PRODUCT

'COMPROMISE' GDP

The quarterly national accounts, appearing in *Economic Trends* for January, April, July and October of each year, provide four estimates, in one form or another, of gross domestic product. Of these, two (output and expenditure) are at constant prices, and two (income and expenditure) at current prices. On the assumption that the relationship between expenditure estimates at current and at constant prices gives an unbiased estimate of the overall price deflator, it is thus possible to form three independent estimates of real GDP:

real output (given)
real expenditure (given)
real income (money income × real expenditure/money expenditure)

Of these, real output is in the form of an index number, the remainder in £ millions at 1963 prices. The output index may be converted to money terms by basing it on the average of income and expenditure measures in the base year.

The problem now arises: which measure, or combination of measures, provides the best estimate of what really happened. There would be no difficulty if all three moved precisely together, but this is true in neither the long nor the short term. There is no reason to suppose that any of the measures is inherently more accurate than the others and, in an early examination of the problem, Godley and Gillion suggested the use of a simple arithmetic average of the three measures as the best compromise estimate on which to base analysis and forecasts.[1]

A more formal statistical analysis of the problem has been conducted by Black and Kidgell.[2] It is assumed that each of the three measures consists of two components – true GDP and a random error. Making the (strong) assumption that each of the three random errors has equal variance, and also assuming that they are independent, it can be shown that the first principal component of the three series is the linear combination which has minimum variance about the true value of GDP. The statistical analysis shows that, both in terms of levels and of changes, the 'best' combination gives very nearly equal weights to the three measures, thus to some extent confirming the informal procedure of Godley and Gillion.

[1] W. A. H. Godley and C. Gillion, 'Measuring national product', *National Institute Economic Review*, No. 27, February 1964.

[2] I. G. Black and J. E. Kidgell, 'A compromise estimate of GDP' in Hilton and Heathfield (eds.), *The Econometric Study of the United Kingdom*.

At the same time, it must be admitted that the methods employed by the national income accounts statisticians cast considerable doubt on the validity of the assumptions of equal variance and independence of the error terms.[1] In the absence of a detailed study of the interrelationships of the various components of the national accounts, it is probably necessary to give the three measures equal weight in arriving at a single compromise measure of GDP more for informal convenience than because of supposed statistical justification.

RECONCILED EXPENDITURES

Having settled on a single measure of GDP for analytic purposes, there is the problem of reconciling the published expenditure components with the compromise GDP total. (The published figures naturally add up to expenditure and not to compromise GDP.) The difference between compromise and expenditure measures of GDP must be regarded as unrecorded expenditure. In practice, most if not all of this discrepancy is treated as unrecorded stockbuilding. There are two reasons for this. First, stockbuilding is the least reliable of the expenditure estimates.[2] Secondly, when the discrepancy is included as an independent variable in import functions (see chapter 4), its regression coefficient implies an import content closer to that of stockbuilding than to that of other kinds of expenditure (though this might, of course, indicate that the discrepancy in part represents unrecorded imports).

The evidence for the attribution of the discrepancy, however, remains weak, and in the analysis of the behavioural relationships described in earlier chapters, recorded expenditure series have been used in general, entailing a slight, though almost certainly insignificant, inconsistency. In forecasting, 'reconciled' expenditure figures are used, so that a consistent expenditure table can be presented.

[1] *National Accounts Statistics – Sources and Methods.*
[2] *Ibid.*, p. 42.

APPENDIX II

PARAMETERS OF THE MODEL

There is no single version which can be given as *the* model used in forecasting at the National Institute. The re-estimation of relationships as new data appear and the investigation of new relationships are continuing processes. Nevertheless, the essential structure has remained much the same and the form given below conveys a reasonable picture of the sizes of the various parameters. This form has been chosen to be given in full principally because it is one version with which extensive simulation studies were carried out. It is these studies on which the latter part of chapter 8 is based.

The symbols are defined on page viii and, as before, italics indicate current prices and bold type exogenous variables. Each behavioural equation contains an intercept adjustment term (see chapter 8), written as, for example, 'RESIRSE' for the income from rent and self-employment (IRSE) equation. Throughout 'log' means natural logarithm and 'exp' means exponential.

Behavioural equations

1. Income from rent and self-employment

$$\mathit{IRSE} = \boldsymbol{\mathit{RESIRSE}} + \exp(-1{\cdot}006 + 0{\cdot}2022 \log \mathrm{GDP} + 0{\cdot}8854 \log \mathit{IRSE}_{-1})$$

2. Income from dividends and net interest receipts

$$\mathit{DNI} = \boldsymbol{\mathit{RESDNI}} + \exp(-11{\cdot}335 + 1{\cdot}78685 \log \mathrm{GDP} + 0{\cdot}2983 \log \mathit{DNI}_{-1})$$

3. Wage and salary bill

$$\mathit{WS} = \boldsymbol{\mathit{RESWS}} + \exp(-0{\cdot}14477 + 0{\cdot}355744 \log \mathrm{GDP} + 0{\cdot}645874 \log \mathit{WS}_{-1} + 0{\cdot}0027781\, \mathbf{TIM})$$

4. Tax on wages and salaries

$$\mathit{TAXWS} = \boldsymbol{\mathit{RESTAXWS}} - 583 + (0{\cdot}24 + 0{\cdot}001\, \mathbf{TIM})\, \mathit{WS}$$

5. Other personal tax

$$\mathit{TAXO} = \boldsymbol{\mathit{RESTAXO}} - 301 + 0{\cdot}33\, \mathit{IRSE} + 0{\cdot}4\, \mathit{DNI}$$

6. Non-credit consumption

$$\mathrm{CEND} = \mathbf{RESCEND} + 269 + 0{\cdot}4719\, \mathrm{RDW} + 0{\cdot}4\, \mathrm{RDO} + 0{\cdot}449\, \mathrm{CEND}_{-1}$$

7. Consumer price index (excluding indirect taxes)

$$\mathrm{CPIFC} = \mathbf{RESCPIFC} + 0{\cdot}3183\, \mathit{WS}/\mathrm{GDP} + 0{\cdot}046\, \mathbf{MP} + 0{\cdot}7623\, \mathrm{CPIFC}_{-1}$$

8. Factor cost adjustment

$$\Delta\, \mathrm{FCA} = \mathbf{RESFCA} - 2 + 0{\cdot}309\, \Delta \mathrm{CE}$$

9. Stocks (level)

$$S = \mathbf{RESS} + 216 + 0{\cdot}35245\ \mathrm{GDP} - 0{\cdot}171\ (\Delta \mathrm{TFS} - \Delta \mathrm{FCA}) + 0{\cdot}77228\ S_{-1}$$

10. Imports of goods and services

$$\mathrm{IMP} = \mathbf{RESIMP} - 421 + 0{\cdot}322\ \mathrm{INV} + 0{\cdot}2128\ \mathrm{TFS}$$

Identities

11. Consumer price index

$$\mathrm{CPI} = 0{\cdot}856\ \mathrm{CPIFC} + 0{\cdot}144\ \mathbf{T}$$

12. Real disposable wage income

$$\mathrm{RDW} = [\mathit{WS} + \boldsymbol{FP} + (\boldsymbol{ERC} - \boldsymbol{EEC}) + 1{\cdot}1\ \boldsymbol{CG} - \mathit{TAXWS}]/\mathrm{CPI}$$

13. Other real disposable income

$$\mathrm{RDO} = (\mathit{IRSE} + \mathit{DNI} - \boldsymbol{NTA} - \mathit{TAXO})/\mathrm{CPI}$$

14. Consumers' expenditure

$$\mathrm{CE} = \mathrm{CEND} + (\Delta\ \boldsymbol{CR})/\mathrm{CPI}$$

15. Total final sales

$$\mathrm{TFS} = \mathrm{CE} + \mathbf{PAC} + \mathbf{GFI} + \mathbf{EX}$$

16. Stockbuilding

$$\mathrm{INV} = S - S_{-1}$$

17. Gross domestic product

$$\mathrm{GDP} = \mathrm{TFS} + \mathrm{INV} - \mathrm{IMP} - \mathrm{FCA}$$

It will be noted that the model does not generate paths for employment and unemployment. These are obtained from the GDP projection outside the model by means of the type of relationship described in chapter 7. The employment path so derived provides, in conjunction with the forecast wage and salary bill, an implicit projection of earnings per head.

APPENDIX III

THE COMPUTER PROGRAMME FOR SOLVING THE MODEL

The following computer programme (table 9), which uses a later version of the model than that given in appendix II above, was developed at the Institute to perform the calculations necessary for the solution of the model, using the Gauss-Seidel method for solution of systems of non-linear simultaneous equations.[1] The programme is written in 'Basic' – one of the languages used by companies operating the 'time-sharing' system.

Table 9. *Computer programme for solving the model*

```
  5 FILES ENDOG; EXOG; FORCAT
  7 DIM X (21, 16), E(15), Y(15,16), A$(15)
 10 READ N1, N5, N2, N6, N4, N7, A
 11 DATA 15, 8, 21, 16, 9, 16
 12 DATA 1
 15 FOR I = 1 TO N1
 20 READ #1, A$(I)
 25 FOR J = 1 TO N5
 30 READ #1, Y(I,J)
 35 NEXT J
 40 NEXT I
 42 FOR I = 1 TO N2
 45 READ #2, X$
 50 FOR J = 1 TO N6
 55 READ #2, X(I,J)
 58 NEXT J
 60 NEXT I
 62 FOR K = N4 TO N7 [a]
 63 FOR I = 1 TO N1
 70 LET Y(I,K) = Y(I,K-1)
 75 NEXT I
 80 LET M = 0
 88 LET M = M + 1 [b]
 90 IF M < 40 THEN 100
 92 PRINT M; 'ITS NEW VALUE FOR A';
 94 INPUT A
 96 IF A = 0 THEN 999
 98 GO TO 63
100 LET V1 = -·82987 + ·16014*LOG[Y(14,K)] + ·91472*LOG[Y(1,K-1)
                 - X(12,K-1)] [c]
105 LET Y(1,K) = EXP(V1) + X(12,K)
```

[1] See pp. 74–5.

```
120 LET V2 = -11·7652 + 1·86858*LOG[Y(14,K)] + ·25175*LOG[Y(2,K-1)
        — X(13,K-1)]
125 LET Y(2,K) = EXP(V2) + X(13,K)
130 LET E(3) = -Y(3,K) — 260 + ·33*Y(1,K) + ·4*Y(2,K) + X(14,K)
131 LET Y(3,K) = Y(3,K) + A*E(3)
135 LET V3 = [Y(1,K) + Y(2,K) – X(7,K) – Y(3,K)]/[·01*Y(9,K)]
140 LET V4 = ·18502 + ·29618*LOG[Y(14,K)] + ·66955*LOG[Y(4,K-1) – X(15,K-1)]
143 LET E(4) = -Y(4,K) + EXP[V4 + ·00299*X(11,K)] + X(15,K)
147 LET Y(4,K) = Y(4,K) + A*E(4)
150 LET E(5) = –Y(5,K) – 168 + [·159 + ·001*X(11,K)]*Y(4,K) + X(16,K)
155 LET Y(5,K) = Y(5,K) + A*E(5)
158 LET V5 = [Y(4,K) + X(5,K) + X(6,K) – Y(5,K) + 1·1*X(8,K)]/[·01*Y(9,K)]
159 LET V6 = Y(6,K-1) – X(17,K-1)
160 LET E(6) = -Y(6,K) + 239 + ·3395*V6 + ·601*V5 + ·4*V3 + X(17,K)
163 LET Y(6,K) = Y(6,K) + A*E(6)
170 LET Y(7,K) = Y(6,K) + X(10,K)/[·01*Y(9,K)]
180 LET E(8) = -Y(8,K) + 1·31024 + 31·5015*Y(4,K)/Y(14,K) + ·034786*X(4,K)
181 LET E(8) = E(8) + ·762514*[Y(8,K-1) – X(18,K-1)]
183 LET E(8) = E(8) + X(18,K)
187 LET Y(8,K) = Y(8,K) + A*E(8)
190 LET Y(9,K) = ·856*Y(8,K) + ·144*X(9,K)
200 LET Y(10,K) = X(1,K) + X(2,K) + X(3,K) + Y(7,K)
210 LET V7 = ·145*Y(7,K) + ·03*X(3,K) + ·027*X(1,K) + ·053*X(2,K)
        + ·012*Y(12,K)
211 LET V7 = V7 – ·145*Y(7,K-1) – ·03*X(3,K-1) – ·027*X(1,K-1) – ·053*X(2,K-1)
212 LET V7 = V7 – ·012*Y(12,K-1)
213 LET E(11) = -Y(11,K) + Y(11,K-1) – X(19, K-1) – 4·1 + 2*V7
214 LET E(11) = E(11) + X(19,K)
215 LET Y(11,K) = Y(11,K) + A*E(11)
220 LET Y (12,K) = Y(15,K) – Y(15,K-1)
230 LET E(13) = – Y(13,K) – 448 + ·304*Y(12,K) + ·215*Y(10,K) + X(21,K)
235 LET Y(13,K) = Y(13,K) + A*E(13)
240 LET Y(14,K) = Y(10,K) + Y(12,K) – Y(13,K) – Y(11,K)
250 LET E(15) = -Y(15,K) + 268 + ·3426*Y(14,K) + ·773*[Y(15,K-1) – X(20,K-1)]
252 LET E(15) = E(15) – ·195* [Y(10,K) – Y(10,K–1) – Y(11,K) + (Y11,K–1)]
253 LET E(15) = E(15) + X(20,K)
255 LET Y(15,K) = Y(15,K) + A*E(15) [c]
405 FOR I = 1 TO N1
410 IF ABS[E(I)/Y(I,K)]>·0001 THEN 88 [b]
415 NEXT I
425 NEXT K [a]
430 PRINT
435 SCRATCH #3
440 FOR I = 1 TO N1
445 WRITE #3, A$(I);
455 FOR J = 1 TO N7
460 WRITE #3, Y(I,J);
465 NEXT J
470 NEXT I
989 CHAIN PRINT
999 STOP
```

[a] The solution period loop connects line 62 with line 425.
[b] The iteration loop connects line 88 with line 410.
[c] The model itself is contained in lines 100–255 inclusive.

Chart 5. *Simplified flow chart of model solution programme*

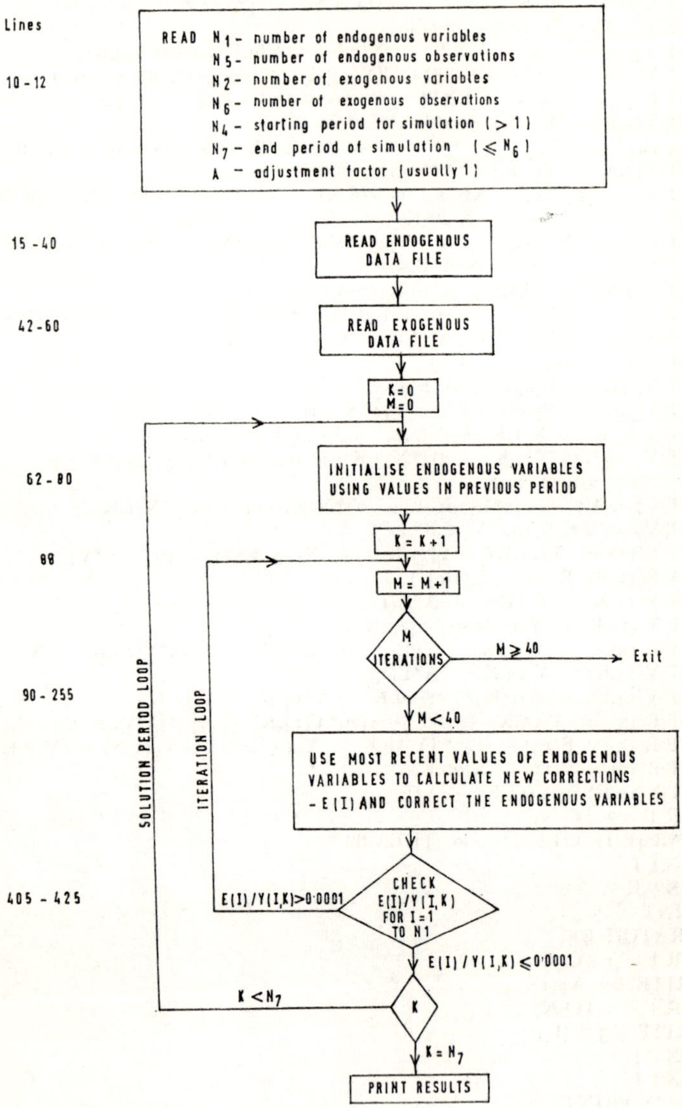

The programme is probably self-explanatory if read in conjunction with chart 5 and the section on the solution of the model in chapter 8.[1] However the following notes may also be helpful:

[1] See pp. 74–6.

Table 10. *A data file: ENDOG for 1969–70*

10	*IRSE*
11	1073 1083 1098 1120 1138 1168 1190
12	1215
20	*DNI*
21	785 771 753 784 731 845 812
22	800
30	*TAXO*
31	354 372 396 410 425 470 480
32	475
40	*WS*
41	5875 5955 6075 6280 6405 6640 6890
42	7140
50	*TAXWS*
51	895 896 926 957 981 1054 1052
52	1150
60	CEND
61	5594 5672 5707 5738 5708 5776 5815
62	5871
70	CE
71	5580 5653 5683 5713 5722 5820 5852
72	5890
80	CPIFC
81	119·1 119·8 121·2 122·6 123·7 125·8 128·2
82	131·1
90	CPI
91	124·3 125·7 127·1 128·7 129·9 132 134·1
92	136·6
100	TFS
101	10590 10753 10905 10953 10915 11134 11160
102	11239
110	FCA
111	1033 1058 1076 1085 1082 1110 1153
112	1150
120	INV
121	115 73 37 68 19 65 129
122	77
130	IMP
131	1910 1939 1934 1972 1991 2073 2089
132	2126
140	GDP
141	7762 7829 7932 7964 7861 8016 8047
142	8040
150	S
151	12730 12803 12840 12908 12927
152	12992 13121 13198

1. Three other files are used in conjunction with the solution programme (line 5). ENDOG and EXOG contain the recent and (in EXOG) the forecast values of the endogenous and exogenous variables respectively.

SYMBOLS: see pp. xi, xii.

The third file, FORCAT, is a blank file into which all values (including the forecasts) of the endogenous variables are fed (lines 440–70) after solutions have been calculated for the specified number of periods. These values are then carried over into another programme (PRINT) at line 989. This programme merely organises all the information and prints it out in the precise form of the tables (for GDP and personal income and expenditure) which appear in the *Economic Review*.[1]

2. Definition of the arrays (line 7):
   The X (I, J) array contains all the exogenous variables followed by the values of the residuals (intercept adjustments, see pages 72–4 above), both for the recent past and for the forecast period.
   Y contains the recent observations of the endogenous variables and, when all the solutions have been calculated, their forecast values.
   A$ contains the names of the endogenous variables.
   The changes in the values of the endogenous variables (the errors at each iteration) are put into E.

3. The programme incorporates a check (lines 90–6) which stops the computation if convergence to a solution has not been achieved after 40 iterations. Convergence is deemed to have been achieved when the correction applied to any endogenous variable is not greater than 0·01 per cent.

4. An example of one of the data files (which are prepared and fed in separately) is given in table 10. The same format is used in preparing the exogenous data file, although this contains values for the forecast period too.

[1] See for example *National Institute Economic Review*, No. 55, February 1971, tables 1, 5 and 6, pp. 23, 27 and 29.

INDEX

PUBLICATIONS OF THE NATIONAL INSTITUTE OF ECONOMIC AND SOCIAL RESEARCH

published by

THE CAMBRIDGE UNIVERSITY PRESS

Books published for the Institute by the Cambridge University Press are available through ordinary booksellers. They appear in the three series below.

ECONOMIC & SOCIAL STUDIES

*I *Studies in the National Income, 1924–1938*
Edited by A. L. BOWLEY. Reprinted with corrections, 1944. pp. 256.

*II *The Burden of British Taxation*
By G. FINDLAY SHIRRAS and L. ROSTAS. 1942. pp. 140.

*III *Trade Regulations and Commercial Policy of the United Kingdom*
By THE RESEARCH STAFF OF THE NATIONAL INSTITUTE OF ECONOMIC AND SOCIAL RESEARCH. 1943. pp. 275.

*IV *National Health Insurance: A Critical Study*
By HERMAN LEVY. 1944. pp. 356.

*V *The Development of the Soviet Economic System: An Essay on the Experience of Planning in the U.S.S.R.*
By ALEXANDER BAYKOV. 1946. pp. 530.
(Out of print in this series, but reprinted 1970 in Cambridge University Press Library Edition, £5.00 net.)

*VI *Studies in Financial Organization*
By T. BALOGH. 1948. pp. 328.

*VII *Investment, Location, and Size of Plant: A Realistic Inquiry into the Structure of British and American Industries*
By P. SARGANT FLORENCE, assisted by W. BALDAMUS. 1948. pp. 230.

*VIII *A Statistical Analysis of Advertising Expenditure and of the Revenue of the Press*
By NICHOLAS KALDOR and RODNEY SILVERMAN. 1948. pp. 200.

*IX *The Distribution of Consumer Goods*
By JAMES B. JEFFERYS, assisted by MARGARET MACCOLL and G. L. LEVETT. 1950. pp. 430.

*X *Lessons of the British War Economy*
Edited by D. N. CHESTER. 1951. pp. 260.

*XI *Colonial Social Accounting*
By PHYLLIS DEANE. 1953. pp. 360.

*XII *Migration and Economic Growth*
By BRINLEY THOMAS. 1954. pp. 384.

*XIII *Retail Trading in Britain*, 1850–1950
By JAMES B. JEFFERYS. 1954. pp. 490.

*XIV *British Economic Statistics*
By CHARLES CARTER and A. D. ROY. 1954. pp. 192.

XV *The Structure of British Industry: A Symposium*
Edited by DUNCAN BURN. 1958. Vol. I. pp. 403. £2.75 net. Vol. II. pp. 499. £3.15 net.

*XVI *Concentration in British Industry*
By RICHARD EVELY and I. M. D. LITTLE. 1960. pp. 357.

*XVII *Studies in Company Finance*
Edited by BRIAN TEW and R. F. HENDERSON. 1959. pp. 301.

XVIII *British Industrialists: Steel and Hosiery, 1850–1950*
By CHARLOTTE ERICKSON. 1959. pp. 276. £2.25 net.

* At present out of print

XIX *The Antitrust Laws of the U.S.A.: A Study of Competition Enforced by Law*
By A. D. NEALE. 2nd edition, 1970. pp. 544. £4.00 net.

XX *A Study of United Kingdom Imports*
By M. FG. SCOTT. 1963. pp. 270. £3.00 net.

XXI *Industrial Growth and World Trade*
By ALFRED MAIZELS. Reprinted with corrections, 1971. pp. 563. £4.20 net.

XXII *The Management of the British Economy, 1945–60*
By J. C. R. DOW. 1964. pp. 443. £3.00 net.

XXIII *The British Economy in 1975*
By W. BECKERMAN AND ASSOCIATES. 1965. pp.631. £4.00 net.

XXIV *Occupation and Pay in Great Britain, 1906–60*
By GUY ROUTH. 1965. pp. 182. £1.75 net.

XXV *Exports and Economic Growth of Developing Countries*
By A. MAIZELS, assisted by L. F. CAMPBELL-BOROSS and P. B. W. RAYMENT. 1968. pp. 445. £3.00 net.

XXVI *Urban Development in Britain: Standards, Costs and Resources, 1964–2004*
By P. A. STONE.
Vol. 1: *Population Trends and Housing*. 1970. pp. 436. £3.00 net.

OCCASIONAL PAPERS

*I *The New Population Statistics*
By R. R. KUCZYNSKI. 1942. pp. 31.

*II *The Population of Bristol*
By H. A. SHANNON and E. GREBENIK. 1943. pp. 92.

*III *Standards of Local Expenditure*
By J. R. HICKS and U. K. HICKS. 1943. pp. 61.

*IV *War-time Pattern of Saving and Spending*
By CHARLES MADGE. 1943. pp. 139.

*V *Standardized Accounting in Germany*
By H. W. SINGER. Reprinted 1944. pp. 68.

*VI *Ten Years of Controlled Trade in South-Eastern Europe*
By N. MOMTCHILOFF. 1944. pp. 90.

*VII *The Problem of Valuation for Rating*
By J. R. HICKS, U. K. HICKS and C. E. V. LESER. 1944. pp. 90.

*VIII *The Incidence of Local Rates in Great Britain*
By J. R. HICKS and U. K. HICKS. 1945. pp. 64.

*IX *Contributions to the Study of Oscillatory Time-Series*
By M. G. KENDALL. 1946. pp. 76.

*X *A System of National Book-keeping Illustrated by the Experience of the Netherlands Economy*
By J. B. D. DERKSEN. 1946. pp. 34.

*XI *Productivity, Prices and Distribution in Selected British Industries*
By L. ROSTAS. 1948. pp. 199.

*XII *The Measurement of Colonial National Incomes: An Experiment*
By PHYLLIS DEANE. 1948. pp. 173.

*XIII *Comparative Productivity in British and American Industry*
By L. ROSTAS. 1948. pp. 263.

*XIV *The Cost of Industrial Movement*
By W. F. LUTTRELL. 1952. pp. 104.

XV *Costs in Alternative Locations: The Clothing Industry*
By D. C. HAGUE and P. K. NEWMAN. 1952. pp. 73. £1.05 net.

*XVI *Social Accounts of Local Authorities*
By J. E. G. UTTING. 1953. pp. 81.

*XVII *British Post-war Migration*
By JULIUS ISAAC. 1954. pp. 294.

* At present out of print

*XVIII *The Cost of the National Health Service in England and Wales*
By BRIAN ABEL-SMITH and RICHARD M. TITMUSS. 1956. pp. 176.

*XIX *Post-war Investment, Location and Size of Plant*
By P. SARGANT FLORENCE. 1962. pp. 51.

*XX *Investment and Growth Policies in British Industrial Firms*
By TIBOR BARNA. 1962. pp. 71.

XXI *Pricing and Employment in the Trade Cycle: A Study of British Manufacturing Industry, 1950–61*
By R. R. NEILD. 1963. pp. 73. 75p. net.

XXII *Health and Welfare Services in Britain in 1975*
By DEBORAH PAIGE and KIT JONES. 1966. pp. 142. £1.05 net.

XXIII *Lancashire Textiles: A Case Study of Industrial Change*
By CAROLINE MILES. 1968. pp. 124. £1.05 net.

XXIV *The Economic Impact of Commonwealth Immigration*
By K. JONES and A. D. SMITH. 1970. pp. 186. £1.75 net.

STUDIES IN THE NATIONAL INCOME AND EXPENDITURE OF THE UNITED KINGDOM

Published under the joint auspices of the National Institute and the Department of Applied Economics, Cambridge.

*1 *The Measurement of Consumers' Expenditure and Behaviour in the United Kingdom, 1920–1938* vol. I
By RICHARD STONE, assisted by D. A. ROWE and by W. J. CORLETT, RENEE HURSTFIELD, MURIEL POTTER. 1954. pp. 448.

2 *The Measurement of Consumers' Expenditure and Behaviour in the United Kingdom, 1920–1938* vol. II
By RICHARD STONE and D. A. ROWE. 1966. pp. 152. £4.50 net.

3 *Consumers' Expenditure in the United Kingdom, 1900–1919*
By A. R. PREST, assisted by A. A. ADAMS. 1954. pp. 196. £3.15 net.

4 *Domestic Capital Formation in the United Kingdom, 1920–1938*
By C. H. FEINSTEIN. 1965. pp. 284. £4.50 net.

5 *Wages and Salaries in the United Kingdom, 1920–1938*
By AGATHA CHAPMAN, assisted by ROSE KNIGHT. 1953. pp. 254. £4.00 net.

NIESR STUDENTS' EDITION

1 *Growth and Trade* (abridged from *Industrial Growth and World Trade*)
By A. MAIZELS. 1970. pp. 312. £1.05 net.

2 *The Antitrust Laws of the U.S.A.* (2nd edition, unabridged)
By A. D. NEALE. 1970. pp. 544. £1.40 net.

3 *The Management of the British Economy, 1945–60* (unabridged)
By J. C. R. DOW. 1970. pp. 464. £1.10 net.

REGIONAL PAPERS

1 *The Anatomy of Regional Activity Rates* by JOHN BOWERS, and *Regional Social Accounts for the United Kingdom* by V. H. WOODWARD. 1970. pp. 192. £1.25 net.

* At present out of print

THE ANALYSIS AND FORECASTING OF THE BRITISH ECONOMY

M. J. C. SURREY

The National Institute has been engaged in short-term forecasting of the British economy since 1959 when the *National Institute Economic Review* first appeared. In recent years research has aimed at developing more formal forecasting methods so that computer facilities can be used to full advantage. Substantial progress has been made and this book describes the current position.

The framework of analysis is first outlined to convey a general picture of the economy's behaviour; then the major determinants are examined in more detail, with some account of the empirical work on which the relationships are based. The last two chapters describe the use of the formal model and the extent to which informal and intuitive processes still play a part in the 'art' of forecasting. The appendices contain further details of the model including a computer programme for its solution.

Recent N.I.E.S.R. Occasional Papers

CAMBRIDGE UNIVERSITY PRESS

London: Bentley House, 200 Euston Road, London NW1 2DB
New York: 32 East 57th Street, New York 10022
Melbourne: 296 Beaconsfield Parade, Middle Park, Victoria 3206
Sydney: 184 Sussex Street, Sydney, N.S.W. 2000

0 521 09675 9

PRINTED IN GREAT BRITAIN